THEMATIC UNIT

Ancient Japan

Written by Michelle Breyer, M.A.

Teacher Created Materials, Inc.

6421 Industry Way

Westminster, CA 92683

www.teachercreated.com

©*1999 Teacher Created Materials, Inc.*

Made in U.S.A.

ISBN 1-55734-579-1

Edited by

Barbara M. Wally, M.S.

Illustrated by

Bruce Hedges

Cover Art by

Cheri Macoubrie Wilson

Table of Contents

Introduction

Ancient Japan contains a comprehensive whole language, thematic unit. Its 80 reproducible pages are filled with a wide variety of lesson ideas designed for use with intermediate and middle school students. At its core are three high-quality reading selections: *Exploration into Japan*, *The Samurai's Tale*, and *The Sign of the Chrysanthemum*.

For each of these books, activities are included which set the stage for reading, encourage the enjoyment of the book, and extend the concept. Activities are also provided to integrate the theme into the curriculum areas of language arts (including writing and research skills), math, science, social studies, and art. Many of these activities are conducive to the use of cooperative learning groups. Most of the activities may be used with any of the reading selections, should you choose to read only one or two of the books.

Suggestions and patterns for bulletin boards and unit management tools are additional timesavers for the busy teacher. Furthermore, directions for culminating activities such as A Day in Ancient Japan, Conduct a Tea Ceremony, and Famous People and Places allow students to synthesize their knowledge in order to produce products that can be shared beyond the classroom.

This thematic unit includes the following:

❑ **literature selections**—summaries of three books with related lessons that cross the curriculum

❑ **fine arts**—suggestions for activities in music, drama, poetry, and the visual arts

❑ **planning guides**—suggestions for sequencing lessons of the unit

❑ **writing ideas**—a variety of writing suggestions and activities that cross the curriculum

❑ **bulletin boards**—suggestions and plans for content-related and interactive bulletin boards

❑ **home/school connections**—ideas for extending learning into the students homes

❑ **curriculum connections**—activities in language arts, math, science, social studies, and fine arts

❑ **group projects**—activities to foster cooperative learning

❑ **technology**—a listing of Internet sites which can be used to broaden the students' understanding of the unit

❑ **culminating activities**—projects which require students to synthesize their learning and participate in activities that can be shared with others

❑ **a bibliography**—suggestions for additional literature and non-fiction books relating to this unit

Introduction *(cont.)*

Why a Balanced Approach?

The strength of a whole language approach is that it involves children in using all modes of communication—reading, writing, listening, illustrating, and doing. Communication skills are interconnected and integrated into lessons that emphasize the whole of language. Balancing this approach is our knowledge that every whole — including individual words — is composed of parts, and directed study of those parts can help a student to master the whole. Experience and research tell us that regular attention to phonics, other word attack skills, spelling, etc., develops reading mastery, thereby fulfilling the unity of the whole language experience. The child is thus led to read, write, spell, speak, and listen confidently in response to a literature experience introduced by the teacher. In these ways, language skills grow rapidly, stimulated by direct practice, involvement, and interest in the topic at hand.

Why Thematic Planning?

One very useful tool for implementing an integrated whole language program is thematic planning. By choosing a theme with correlating literature selections for a unit of study, a teacher can plan activities throughout the day that lead to a cohesive, in-depth study of the topic. Students will be practicing and applying their skills in meaningful contexts. Consequently, they will tend to learn and retain more. Both teachers and students will be freed from a day that is broken into unrelated segments of isolated drill and practice.

Why Cooperative Learning?

Besides academic skills and content, students need to learn social skills. No longer can this area of development be taken for granted. Students must learn to work cooperatively in groups in order to function well in modern society. Group activities should be a regular part of school life, and teachers should consciously include social objectives as well as academic objectives in their planning. The teacher should clarify and monitor the qualities of good group interaction, just as he/she would clarify and monitor the academic goals of the project.

Why Technology?

Our students are rapidly approaching the real world where knowledge of technological advances is a must. In order for our students to compete outside the classroom, it is necessary for them to have a wide range of technological experiences, including an understanding of word processing, multimedia presentations, video, and computer simulations. Technology also helps motivate students and enhance their learning experience by providing another avenue to gain and report information.

Exploration into Japan

by Richard Tames

Summary

This nonfiction book explores the story of Japan from the early humans of the Jomon culture to the late twentieth century. The book is divided into six sections that provide an overview of the major events and eras in Japanese history. Significant cultural and political developments of each period are highlighted. The book is well illustrated, and includes picture captions and highlighted boxes which give additional information and insight. A time line provides a comparison of Japanese history to events in Europe.

This outline is a suggested plan for using the various activities that are presented in this book. Each of the lessons can take from one to several days to complete.

Sample Plan

Lesson 1

❑ Introduce students to the age of Ancient Japan, page 6.
❑ Make a bulletin board map of Japan and torii gates for your classroom, pages 77–78.
❑ Make organizational folders/journals, page 77.
❑ Introduce the vocabulary lists and activities, pages 7–8.

Lesson 2

❑ Read pages 4–9 of *Exploration into Japan* to learn about the early cultures in Japan.
❑ Complete a vocabulary activity for this selection, page 8.
❑ Begin a period time line, pages 44–45.
❑ Compare the early Japanese people, page 9.
❑ Make a Jomon pot, page 60.
❑ Read a Japanese creation myth, page 43.
❑ Learn about burial customs in ancient Japan and design your own tomb, pages 15–16.

Lesson 3

❑ Read pages 10–15 of *Exploration into Japan* to examine China's influence on Japan.
❑ Complete a vocabulary activity for this selection, page 8.
❑ Compare Shinto to Buddhism, page 14.
❑ Report on natural resources, page 10.
❑ Write in Japanese, page 42.
❑ Discuss the geographical isolation of Japan, page 11.

Lesson 4

❑ Read pages 10–15 of *Exploration into Japan* to learn about Shoguns and Samurai.
❑ Experience the Zen way of life, pages 12–13.

❑ Create a classroom meditation garden, page 65.
❑ Compare medieval knights and samurai, page 48.
❑ Trace the development of Japanese feudalism, page 47.
❑ Experience a tea ceremony, pages 70–71.

Lesson 5

❑ Read pages 20–29 of *Exploration into Japan* to learn about the unification of Japan.
❑ Complete a vocabulary activity for this selection, page 8.
❑ Write tanka and/or haiku poetry, page 39.
❑ Design a 16th century castle, page 64.
❑ Compare life as a Kyoto courtier or peasant, page 35.

Lesson 6

❑ Read pages 30–37 of *Exploration into Japan* to learn about westernization.
❑ Complete a vocabulary activity for this selection, page 8.
❑ Read and write a Japanese fairy tale, pages 36–38.
❑ Write a persuasive composition on the westernization of Japan, page 40.

Lesson 7

❑ Make a Zen painting, page 66.
❑ Plan a Bunraku puppet show, pages 61–63.
❑ Research and present information on famous people and places, page 72.
❑ Create a day in ancient Japan with food, clothing, drama, art, music, and games, pages 73–76.

Overview of Activities

Setting the Stage

1. Write the following words on a chalkboard: castle, warlords, nobles, peasants, emperor, armor, and feudal states. Ask students, "What culture comes to mind when you see these words? What type of life do you picture?" Discuss responses. Tell students that they will be learning about ancient Japan, and although there are many similarities between life in feudal Japan and feudal Europe, the culture and beliefs differ widely. As a background to the culture, read the page about creating Japan. Refer to the literature book as well as the social studies text throughout the unit.

2. Assemble the Japanese bulletin board (page 77) for students to use as the unit progresses. Make butcher paper torii gates to cover your classroom doorways (page 78). Make organizational folders/journals (page 77) to keep all notes and handouts for reference throughout the unit. Review the vocabulary lists (page 7) and activities (page 8). You may wish to use one activity throughout the entire book or different activities for different reading selections.

Enjoying the Book

1. Begin reading the first section in *Exploration into Japan*. Use the information from these pages to begin a time line of Japan (pages 44–45). Have students research the early humans in the Japanese region (page 9). Discuss how these early hunters and farmers compare with other early cultures around the world. How was water a contributing factor to encourage the growth of civilization?

2. Have students re-create ancient Japanese pots (page 60) and complete a vocabulary activity for words in this reading section.

3. Complete other lessons and activities that correspond to the literature, as mentioned in the Sample Plan on page 5.

Extending the Book

1. The final two sections of this book deal with the westernization of Japan and its role in the twentieth century. While this is not strictly ancient Japan, you may wish to review these events and discuss them in terms of the ancient culture. Would world history be different if Japan had not been isolated for so long? What values and beliefs governed Japan's actions in the two world wars? You may wish to assign individual students to research and report on Japan's role in the modern world, covering topics from leisure to economics.

2. After completing the book, have students write a persuasive composition (page 40) discussing the westernization of Japan and whether it has been beneficial for Japan to open its doors for trade and communication.

3. Review the list of famous people and places (page 72) in Japan. Assign each student a research subject and a time frame for presenting the information to the rest of the class. Students may wish to dress like their characters and bring in visual props for their presentation.

4. As a culmination of this book, create a day in the life of the ancient Japanese (pages 73–76) in which students can eat, dress, and celebrate like they did hundreds of years ago. On this day groups can perform their Noh dramas (page 69) and Bunraku puppet shows (pages 61–63), as well as completing one or more fine arts projects.

Vocabulary Lists

The following words are used in the text and correspond to the lessons in the Sample Plan (page 5).

Lesson 1		**Lesson 2**		**Lesson 3**	
Jomon culture	archipelago	laquer	pagoda	shogun	guilds
archaeologists	mongul	Shinto	province	daimyo	assassinated
Yayoi culture	dogu	Buddhism	calligraphy	samurai	bakufu
emperor	kofun	kami	shingon	bushido	mongol
Ainu people	haniwa			seppuku	Kublai Khan
kanji	glacier			zen	Noh
kana	excavated				
syllabary	migrated				

Lesson 4		**Lesson 5**		**Lesson 6**	
junk	council	kimono	drill	occupation	karaoke
martyrs	namban	sulfurous	parliament	atomic bomb	investment
haiku	beached	conscripts	national diet	tatami	bullet train
persecute	embassy	diplomat	puppet state	geta	calligraphy
fortification	vaccination	consul	aggression	kendo	wood block printing
disciples	imports			ikebana	westernized
cremated	exports			origami	
				bonsai	

Vocabulary Activities

Each reading section contains vocabulary words for the students to study. Below are a few suggestions for activities. Choose one or more activities to use with each group of words.

1. Have students write each word in their journals. After the students locate the word in the story, have them find the definition in a dictionary. Tell the students to write in their journals the definitions that match how the words are used in the book.

2. Have students work in groups to make vocabulary flashcards by writing the sentence from the book that contains the vocabulary word on one side of an index card. On the reverse side write the meaning of the word. Have students quiz each other on their words. Individuals can also use these cards as a self-test.

3. Have individuals make illustrated vocabulary dictionaries by writing each word and its definition on a large index card. Add an illustration to each card. As words are added throughout the reading of the book, keep rearranging the cards into alphabetical order. At the end of the book, bind the cards together, using a hole punch and yarn to make a completed book.

4. Have students make a synonym/antonym chart in their journals. As they write each vocabulary word and sentence from the book, have them also write a synonym for the word that could be substituted into the sentence without changing the meaning. Next, have them write an antonym that changes the meaning of the sentence when substituted for the vocabulary word. Write some of the best synonym sentences on the board to share with the class.

5. Make a parts-of-speech chart in the journal. The headings should include noun, verb, adjective, and adverb. Write the sentence from the book with the vocabulary word highlighted under the proper heading, showing how the word was used in the sentence.

6. Have students use the vocabulary words to write a poem or summary paragraph about those chapters. Highlight the vocabulary words and display some of the best-written pieces.

7. Challenge your students to work with partners to make a vocabulary crossword puzzle, using graph paper. Duplicate some of the best ones to distribute to the class for practice.

8. Conduct a vocabulary bee in your class. Students can play individually or as teams to earn points. Students should give the proper definition of the word after hearing the sentence from the book containing the word. Award extra points for spelling the word correctly.

9. Play vocabulary hide-and-seek by having students work in groups to write the sentence from the book containing the vocabulary word on one index card and the definition of the vocabulary word on another index card. Give one group a designated area to "hide" their cards, and have another group try to "find" the cards and match the words to their definitions.

10. Play vocabulary pictionary or charades by drawing or acting out each vocabulary word.

The Early Japanese Cultures

Write the letter of the early Japanese culture that corresponds to each description. There may be more than one response to a description.

Jomon Culture = J	**Yayoi Culture = Y**	**Tomb Culture = T**

1. _____ This culture centered on hunting, fishing, and gathering.

2. _____ This culture introduced cultivated rice, weaving, and pottery using a potter's wheel. They rode horses and made bronze tools, ornaments, and weapons.

3. _____ This culture built huge keyhole-shaped burial mounds called *kofun* to cover tombs of rulers and nobles.

4. _____ These cultures centered around farming.

5. _____ The earliest record of these people dates back to 8000 B.C.

6. _____ This culture was displaced by people migrating from northeastern Asia by route of Korea around 2,300 years ago.

7. _____ This culture had the most complex social order of the three. Its rulers came from a respected warrior class, and its people were divided into large and small clans.

8. _____ These people used iron to make tools and farm implements.

9. _____ People from this culture made stone, shell, and bone tools, including fishhooks and harpoons.

10. _____ This culture remained isolated from the rest of the world for almost 10,000 years.

11. _____ This culture replaced the Yayoi culture around 200–300 A.D.

12. _____ This culture used clay figures called *haniwa* as guards and servants around tombs.

13. _____ This culture was created by the migrants who displaced the Jomon culture around 300 B.C.

14. _____ The people from this culture settled in the fertile Yamato plain on the largest island, called Honshu.

15. _____ This culture made simple pottery decorated by pushing cords of rope into the wet clay.

Japan's Land and Natural Resources

Unlike most other countries, Japan is a country that consists entirely of islands, and its borders are set by the sea. Refer to a map to complete the following paragraph about the geography of Japan.

Japan consists of four large volcanic islands and more than 4,000 small ones. These islands extend in an irregular crescent from the island of Sakhalin (Russia) to the island of Taiwan.

1._____ is the northernmost island. This island has short summers and severe long winters caused in great part by the northwestern winds blowing from Siberia. The largest of the islands, 2._____, is also called the mainland. Japan's highest and most famous mountain, 3._____, is on this island. The smallest of the main islands, 4._____, is heavily forested and mountainous.

5._____ is the southernmost of the main islands. The summers in the southern parts of Japan are hot and humid, almost subtropical, and the winters are mild with comparatively little snow. The 6._____ which include the Okinawa and Sakashima Islands, are also a part of Japan.

The northern boundary of Japan is 7._____ . The 8._____ forms the eastern and southern borders. The 9._____ also forms part of the southern boundary. To the west, the 10._____ and the 11._____ are the borders.

Activity

The heat and moisture of Japanese summers contribute to the lush vegetation found in Japan. Variations in climate also mean that a wide variety of trees, from subarctic to subtropical, grow in Japan. Only a very small part of Japan's land, about 13 percent, can be used for farming.

On a separate piece of paper, make a five-column chart. Label the columns trees, flowers, animals, birds, and fish. Using encyclopedias and other reference materials, make a list of Japan's plant and animal life. As a class, compare lists. What role did the abundance of plant and animal life play in Japan's isolation?

Extension

Choose one of the main islands, or a group of islands, which are part of the country of Japan. Research your island(s) and prepare a report for the class. Include facts about the topography, significant physical features, and vegetation of your island and any historical events that happened on that island.

An Isolated Land

Work in a small group to discuss the following questions. Use the book, *Exploration into Japan*, and other resource materials to help with your discussion. After you have discussed each question, record your individual response on a separate sheet of paper. Make sure your response is written in complete and well-developed sentences.

Small Group Discussion Questions

1. What geographical features made transportation and trade difficult within Japan? What features made transportation and trade difficult outside of Japan?

2. Because of the difficult terrain, most people in ancient Japan lived and died without ever traveling more than a few miles from their place of birth. Imagine you were born in the city where your school exists. Now imagine that you never left the city limits in your lifetime.

   A. How would your life be different?

   B. What would you be able to do in your area? What would you not be able to do?

   C. What does this tell you about the average lifestyle in ancient Japan?

   D. How far have you traveled in your lifetime? What makes this possible? What does this tell you about available transportation and roadways in ancient Japan?

3. Although Japan rarely traded with other civilizations, they did have communication with China and Korea. Name some of the imports and exports of ancient Japan.

4. Fearing a loss of power, in the 17th century Japan completely shut itself off from the rest of the world. It was against the law to travel abroad or take in immigrants. How do you think this affected their growth of culture? Do you feel it was beneficial or harmful to their success and progress? Explain.

5. How would life be different in your country if it had been shut off from the rest of the world in the 17th century? Think of the history of your nation and how events would have been different with no outside influence.

   A. How would this have affected the growth of democracy?

   B. How would this have affected population growth?

   C. How would this have affected national culture—language, music, dance, dress, etc.?

   D. How would this have affected religion in the nation?

   E. How would this have affected imports, exports, and technology?

   F. Describe what your country would be like today without this external influence.

Home Extension

1. At home, take an inventory of your food, clothing, and possessions. List the items that have come from another nation or from technology produced by another nation.

2. What items (if any) do you have that are produced from plants, animals, and technology native only to your country?

3. Describe what would be missing from your daily life if your country was not open for trade and immigration.

The Zen Way of Life

Buddhism, introduced to Japan by the Chinese and Koreans in the sixth century, had a profound effect on the people of Japan. Of the many different sects or branches of Buddhism, the most influential sect was *Zen*. Zen taught that rigid spiritual and physical discipline would produce an enlightenment of the nature of existence and lead to nirvana. It stressed recognizing the beauty of simplicity and man's harmony within nature. Both meditation and the adherence to defined social rules are components of Zen which are believed to keep peace and harmony within society. This influence can be seen in the fine arts, customs, and daily living habits of the people of Japan today.

Mental Puzzles

Zen masters taught their pupils to reach enlightenment by breaking away from logic. One method was to have students sit and meditate while pondering an impossible question. Try your hand at the following mental questions:

1. What is the sound of one hand clapping?

2. If a tree falls in the forest but no one is near to hear it fall, does it make a sound?

3. What is the length of infinity?

4. What is beyond the edge of the universe?

5. Make a mental question of your own and pose it to a friend.

Process Activities

Zen stressed the importance of the moment. It taught the age-old saying, "Stop to smell roses," or take time to experience the world fully. The emphasis on process can be seen in the arts and ceremonies, such as the Tea Ceremony, developed by Zen priests. Try one or more of the following activities that emphasize "process" rather than "product."

Mixing Paints—Get a Styrofoam egg carton, a paintbrush, a can of water, and red, yellow, blue, and white paints. Fill four of the egg compartments with each of the paints. Using the paintbrush, transfer some paint into an empty compartment and mix with another color. Continue mixing colors in each of the different compartments, washing the brush only when necessary. Try to mix a wide variety of colors in different shades and hues. Remix over other colors as you go. When you decide you are finished, throw the carton away.

Cutting an Apple—The next time you eat an apple, take time to cut the pieces into interesting shapes and sizes. Plan a process for cutting the apple in a different way than usual. Why did you choose this method? Was it more efficient? more interesting? When done, eat the apple.

Take a Walk—Enjoy a walk for the pleasure of walking and observing your surroundings. Do not plan to reach a certain destination or take a particular route. This is not for exercise, so walk slower than usual and feel free to retrace your steps to observe something that interests you. You may walk for miles or only a few hundred feet—it doesn't matter. When you get back home, write down your experience and how this type of walking made you feel.

The Zen Way of Life *(cont.)*

Observation for Meditation

Zen relies on meditation to find tranquility, peace, and harmony. Rock gardens are often found at Zen temples to provide calm, quiet places that emphasize severity, restraint, and simplicity in nature to help one meditate. These places allow people to sit and observe their surroundings so that they might "get into" nature mentally rather than physically. Try the following observation exercises to achieve a state of calm enlightenment:

(Meditation and observation are skills that require practice. Do not get discouraged or scoff at your attempts. The following exercises are great for reducing stress and developing focused concentration that will help you in all of your school subjects!)

Lunchtime Observation: Choose one lunch period to sit by yourself away from your usual crowd. Plan on taking at least ten minutes for your observation. Try to focus only on your sense of sight and not the sounds or smells around you. First examine your environment—the arrangements of tables and seats, the shape of the dining area, and any elements of nature in your surroundings. Note the colors you observe and how the colors interplay with each other. Note the different elements of light and shadow. Then watch what is happening around you. Try to look at the entire group of people acting as a whole. Then try to find the individual groups within the whole. Choose a few individuals to observe as individuals. After the lunch period is over, take time to record your observations, thoughts, and feelings about the exercise.

Sculpture or Object Observation: Choose a sculpture, painting, flower arrangement, or other object to observe for ten minutes. Find a comfortable place to sit with the object in plain view. Focus on your sense of sight and tune out all noises. You are going to try to "feel" the object with your eyes. First, observe the individual parts of the object as if you are very close. Begin at one point on the object and slowly move your focus across the object. Try to note the smooth or rough points. Observe the different colors, the way the light reflects off the surface, and any imperfections. Then observe the object as a whole. Squint at the object so that you can focus on the outlining shape. Note the areas of light and dark, curves and straight lines, and exterior shape and size. If examining a painting, observe the choice of frame for the painting and how it enhances the shape and colors of the art. Squint your eyes to get an image of color only. Note the areas of light and dark. How did the artist balance the areas on the canvas with color and light? Look at the placement of objects in the painting. How do these objects balance each other? Mentally climb inside the painting as if you were there. What could you touch? What would you do? What is the overall feeling the painting gives to you? Now look at the individual parts of the painting separately. Mentally "touch" each of the different components in the painting and see each component as a separate work of art. If possible, look very closely at the painting so that you can see the individual brush strokes and so that it doesn't look like a picture at all, but just blobs of paint. After ten minutes of observation, take time to record your observations, thoughts, and feelings about the exercise.

Other Subjects for Observation: Use the same procedures mentioned above to observe a garden, your face in the mirror, or the sky. Once you have mastered observation, try to focus only on your sense of hearing by closing your eyes and listening to a piece of music, listening to nature and the weather outside, or listening to a crowded room. After each of your observation exercises, record your thoughts and feelings as well as what you observed.

Compare Shinto and Buddhism

Place each letter in the appropriate section of the Venn diagram.

A. Worshippers believed in many gods.

B. *Kami* is the name given to the gods or spirits that exist in nature.

C. This religion emphasizes gaining harmony with nature.

D. This religion believes that *Bodhisattvas*, or saints, help others reach enlightenment.

E. This was the original religion of Japan.

F. This teaches the laws of karma and reincarnation.

G. No founder or prophet of this religion is known.

H. This religion is based on the teachings of Gautama.

I. This religion is called "the way of the gods."

J. Natural wonders are often marked as sacred places with shrines.

K. The first Japanese books recorded myths sacred to this tradition.

L. This religion was imported from China and Korea, although it originated in India.

M. Many different sects exist, including the Pure Land Sect, Lotus Sect, Zen, and Shingon.

N. Temples are run by monks who also acted as warriors in ancient times.

O. Part of this religion honors ancestors and heroes.

P. People purify themselves by washing hands and mouths before entering the shrine.

Q. Followers meditate to reach peace and harmony.

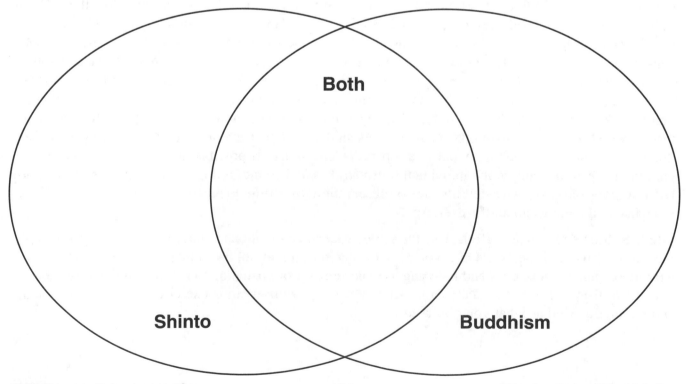

Death in Ancient Japan

The tomb, or *kofun*, period in Japanese history marks the transition from the Yayoi period to the Yamato period, ruled by emperors. Archaeologists have uncovered tombs of the late Yayoi period constructed as simple circular mounds of earth with a wooden coffin placed in a trench near the top. The ruling class then developed more elaborate burial mounds in the shape of a keyhole called *kofun*. The early keyhole tombs were often cut off at the end of a hill or built on the slopes. Later, tombs were built on the plains and are unbelievably impressive monuments to the power and position of their builders.

It was not until the invention of airplanes that many of these tombs were discovered and understood since the majority blended in with the natural features of the landscape. It is now known that as many as 20,000 of these tombs are scattered across the islands of Japan. The grandest of these tombs are attributed to early emperors, with the largest belonging to Emperor Nintoku. This keyhole-shaped tomb is surrounded by three moats, and outside these are thirteen smaller accompanying tombs. The tomb covers about eighty acres, compared to the thirteen acres used for the Great Pyramid in Egypt.

Stone chambers were built inside the tombs to house the large *sarcophagi*, or immense stone coffins. The sarcophagus was first arranged in position, and then a tight-fitting chamber was built around it. The oldest type of sarcophagus resembled a hollowed-out log while later examples have curved outlines resembling a boat. A sloping lid was added to form a shape like a house. A headrest was carved into the floor to add the appearance of comfort for the dead. Imperial bodies were dressed in armor made from iron slats tied together with leather thongs. A complete suit covered the entire body from head to toe. However, a more common burial costume consisted of an iron breastplate that covered the chest. These costumes reinforce the idea that a new warrior-style ruling class had come into power.

Grave goods, including bronze mirrors, jewelry, pottery, tools, weapons, horse riding equipment, and armory were placed in the tomb for the deceased. All kinds of beautiful beads of colored stone and glass were also buried with the dead. Many of these beads were thought to have come from the Sun Goddess and to offer protection in death. These personal possessions were placed in the sarcophagus, around it on the stone-paved floor, or on stone shelves near to the dead. Mirrors and swords, sacred symbols of Japan from the early creation story, were arranged around the body as if forming a ring of protection.

Outside the tombs, on the tops and sides of the burial mounds sat rows of effigies, or *haniwa*, made of unglazed red clay. These were large models of animals, birds, boats, houses, and people that acted as guards and servants. Each figure was fashioned with a tube or projection underneath so that it could be pressed into the ground and stand firmly. The size and simplicity of the haniwa allow them to be seen from a great distance. Archaeologists are still uncertain about the origin and significance of the figures. Some accounts claim the effigies were carved to replace human beings that were buried up to their necks in the ground and left to die when the emperor was entombed. The victims died slowly, and their wailing and moaning disturbed the countryside so that when the empress died a few years later, haniwa were made to replace the humans.

Like the great pharaohs in the pyramids, the early emperors of the tomb period were buried months or even years after their deaths. The emperors planned and built these vast tombs during their lifetimes, partly to visualize in what sort of grandeur they would permanently lie. The period after death and before burial was used to finish the work, to conduct the mourning ceremonies, and to collect the articles to be placed in the tomb. These great tombs of the past still stand as a tribute to the building achievements of the ancient Japanese.

Death in Ancient Japan *(cont.)*

Create Your Own Kofun

Use a sheet of large construction paper, pencil, markers, and crayons to create an ancient Japanese burial mound for yourself, as if you were a famous Japanese emperor. Use a separate sheet of writing paper to describe each feature of your gravesite.

1. In the corner, draw and label a small aerial map of your kofun with the keyhole-shaped mound and moats. Describe the size of the tomb area, the number of moats, and any other outstanding features of your burial grounds.

2. Draw and label a large mound on the paper with rows of haniwa standing guard. Describe the different clay effigies, what they represent, and their roles on your tomb.

3. Under the large mound draw and label your stone burial chamber. Describe the meanings and purposes of the personal items placed in the chamber.

4. Inside the chamber, draw and label your sarcophagus and body. Describe the shape of your sarcophagus and its meaning. Describe your burial costume and any items placed within the sarcophagus.

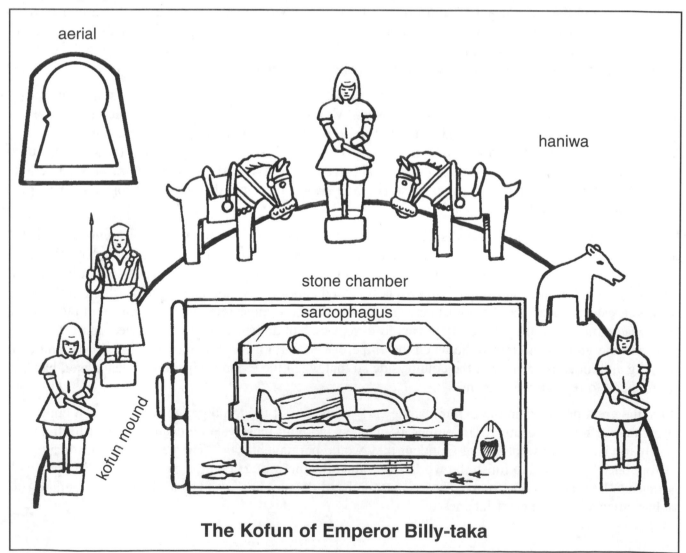

aerial

haniwa

stone chamber

sarcophagus

kofun mound

The Kofun of Emperor Billy-taka

The Samurai's Tale

by Erik Christian Haugaard

Summary

A rival lord takes the four-year-old son of a samurai into custody after killing the boy's family and servants. The boy is given a servant name, Taro, and sent to work in the lord's kitchen. Throughout this well-written and riveting story, Taro struggles with his desire to regain his samurai status. Ancient geography, historical figures, culture, art, religion, and customs are described as the reader follows Taro from kitchen helper to stable boy to messenger and "rice master." Set against the landscape of 16th century feudal Japan, the themes of honor and loyalty resound in this tale of civil war between rival clans surrounding Taro's growth from a helpless child to a trusted samurai teen.

This outline is a suggested plan for using the various activities that are presented in this book. Each of the lessons can take from one to several days to complete.

Sample Plan

Lesson 1
- ❏ Introduce students to the feudal period of Japan, page 47.
- ❏ Make a time line focusing on the feudal period, pages 44–45.
- ❏ Compare a samurai to a knight, page 48.
- ❏ Learn about the changing social order in ancient Japan, page 47.
- ❏ Make a literature journal, page 77.
- ❏ Review the vocabulary activities, page 8.

Lesson 2
- ❏ Read the preface through Chapter 4 of *The Samurai's Tale*.
- ❏ Assign journal and vocabulary activities for this section.
- ❏ Write about someone who has affected your life, page 23.
- ❏ Evaluate Japanese proverbs, page 41.
- ❏ Experiment with the Zen way of life, pages 12–13.
- ❏ Make a family mon, page 67

Lesson 3
- ❏ Read chapters 5–8 of *The Samurai's Tale*.
- ❏ Assign journal and vocabulary activities for this section.
- ❏ Make a time line of life, page 24.
- ❏ Write in Japanese, page 42.
- ❏ Compose tanka and haiku poetry page 39.
- ❏ Compare Shinto and Buddhism, page 14.

Lesson 4
- ❏ Read chapters 9–11 of *The Samurai's Tale*.
- ❏ Assign journal and vocabulary activities for this section.
- ❏ Make a Japanese screen or fan, page 68.
- ❏ Research Japan's geography and environment, page 10.
- ❏ Write about delivering a message, page 24.
- ❏ Predict your future life, page 25.

Lesson 5
- ❏ Read chapters 12–15 of *The Samurai's Tale*.
- ❏ Assign journal and vocabulary activities for this section.
- ❏ Choose a new name, page 25.
- ❏ Tell time in Japanese style, page 59.

Lesson 6
- ❏ Read chapters 16–19 of *The Samurai's Tale*.
- ❏ Assign journal and vocabulary activities for this section.
- ❏ Examine Japanese proverbs, page 26.
- ❏ Learn about ancient social customs, pages 49–51.

Lesson 7
- ❏ Read chapters 20–23 of *The Samurai's Tale*.
- ❏ Assign journal and vocabulary activities for this section.
- ❏ Play a Japanese strategy game, page 58.
- ❏ Design a Japanese castle, page 64.

Lesson 8
- ❏ Read chapters 24–27 of *The Samurai's Tale*.
- ❏ Assign journal and vocabulary activities for this section.
- ❏ Make a Zen painting, page 66.
- ❏ Conduct a tea ceremony, pages 70–71.

Lesson 9
- ❏ Read chapters 28–31 of *The Samurai's Tale*.
- ❏ Assign journal and vocabulary activities for this section.
- ❏ Describe Taro's abundance of fathers, page 27.
- ❏ Read and write a Japanese fairy tale, pages 36–38.

Lesson 10
- ❏ Read chapters 32–34 of *The Samurai's Tale*.
- ❏ Assign journal and vocabulary activities for this section.
- ❏ Write an epilogue, page 27.
- ❏ Plan a Bunraku puppet show (pages 61–63) or Noh play (page 69) to depict a chapter.
- ❏ Complete one or more of the culminating activities for the unit, pages 70–76
- ❏ Assign further reading on the subject, pages 19 and 79.

Overview of Activities

Setting the Stage

1. Introduce students to the Feudal period of Japan by following the steps on page 6. Have students further investigate this time by making a time line (pages 44–45) and comparing a samurai to a knight (page 48). Make sure students understand the feudal system by completing the activity on page 47.

2. Assemble the Japanese bulletin board (page 77) for students to use as the unit progresses. Make organizational folders/journals (page 77) containing the Vocabulary Lists (page 20), Story Map (page 22), Character Chart (page 21), and Examples of Honor and Loyalty (page 23) to use throughout the unit. Review the different vocabulary activities on page 8. You may wish to use one activity throughout the entire length of the book or to use different activities for different reading selections.

3. Before reading the book, have students imagine the horror of having to hide in a trunk while their entire family is slaughtered. Imagine the feelings you would have at only four years of age and how you would react to the situation. What would you do when you emerged from the trunk to face the assassins? What would you do as you were taken from your home with no possessions or clothes? Compare your feelings to those of the main character of the story and note how Japanese culture shaped the reactions of the hero.

Enjoying the Book

1. Begin reading the first selection in *The Samurai's Tale*. Discuss the fate of the main character and predict his future. Have students complete a vocabulary activity in their journals and mark Taro's journey on their story maps. Discuss each character as he or she is introduced in the book and ask the students to write a description on the character chart in their journals. Look for and record examples of honor and loyalty in each selection and discuss their importance to the theme of the book. How do the Japanese culture and codes of conduct restrict Taro's behavior? How do these codes of conduct bring order to the feudal way of life?

2. Follow the sample plan to complete other cross-curricular activities while you continue through the book. Make time to discuss each reading selection and the ongoing journal activities.

Extending the Book

1. After completing the book, have students write an epilogue (page 27) to help define the last line of the book. Share their compositions and compare their predictions for the future.

2. Have groups of students prepare a Bunraku puppet show (pages 61–63) or Noh play (page 69) to reenact different reading selections. Choose one or more of the culminating activities (page 70–76) to finish the unit.

3. For further reading, have students check out the sequel to *The Samurai's Tale* or other fascinating novels about ancient Japan. See the annotated bibliography on page 19 or the bibliography on page 79 for suggestions.

Further Reading Selections

Enjoy some of these other works of historical fiction about medieval Japan.

Dalkey, Kara. *Little Sister* (Harcourt Brace, 1996).
A thirteen-year-old daughter of a noble family in the imperial court of twelfth century Japan enlists the helps of a shape-shifter and other figures from Japanese mythology in her efforts to save her older sister's life.

Haugaard, Erik Christian. *The Boy and the Samurai* (Houghton Mifflin, 1991).
Having grown up as an orphan of the streets while sixteenth century Japan is being ravaged by civil war, a young boy seeks to help a samurai rescue his wife from imprisonment by a warlord so they can all flee to a more peaceful life.

Haugaard, Erik Christian. *The Revenge of the Forty-Seven Samurai* (Houghton Mifflin, 1995).
A fourteen-year-old boy finds himself surrounded by suspicion and betrayal as his master gathers a group of samurai to avenge Lord Asano's death.

Paterson, Katherine. *The Master Puppeteer* (Crowell, 1975).
A thirteen year old boy describes the poverty and discontent of eighteenth century Osaka and the world of Bunraku puppeteers in which he lives.

Paterson, Katherine. *Of Nightingales That Weep* (Crowell, 1974).
The vain young daughter of a samurai finds her comfortable life ripped apart when opposing warrior clans begin a struggle for imperial control of Japan.

San Souci, Robert D. *The Samurai's Daughter* (Dial Books for Young Readers, 1992).
This Japanese folk tale of the Oki Islands is about the brave daughter of a samurai warrior and her journey to be reunited with her exiled father.

Vocabulary Lists

Preface–Chapter 4	Chapters 12–15	Chapters 24–27
bushi	sagely	betrothed
samurai	curs	maliciously
ruthless	vassals	calligraphy
submissively	campaign	retinue
irksome	konidatai	homage
riff-raff	forlornly	contemplated
rabble	hempen	groped
province	majestically	exquisite
tormentor	subservience	aspirations
succor		deigned

Chapters 5–8	Chapters 16–19	Chapters 28–31
dignity	skirmishes	expeditions
prestige	detain	boisterous
tyrannize	pompously	strenuous
meekly	sallied	melancholy
sullenly	besieged	harassed
hara-kiri	cajoled	vanquished
seppuku	ninja	crucify
reverence		
ronins		
scrutinized		
sake		

Chapters 9–11	Chapters 20–23	Chapters 32–34
lucrative	prudence	vigorous
bestowed	sortie	disdainfully
admonished	impregnable	grotesque
vouch	amiss	dilapidated
miso soup	fleeing	
lacquer ware	exploits	
brazier	missive	
	hearsay	
	vanquished	
	refuge	
	humility	
	insubordination	

Character Chart

Use the boxes below to record a description of each character and his or her relation to others as the story unfolds.

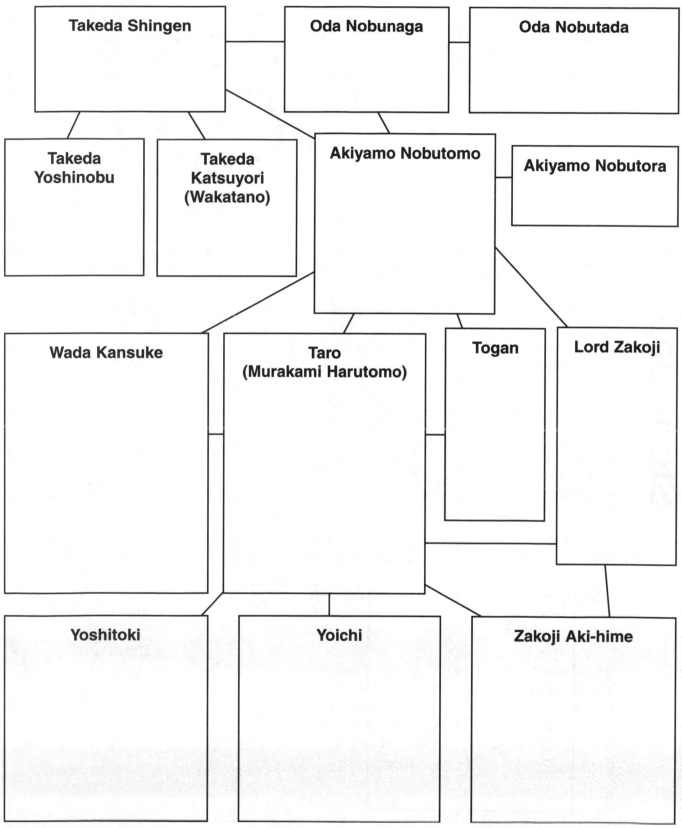

Story Map

Trace the path of Taro as he travels throughout feudal Japan.

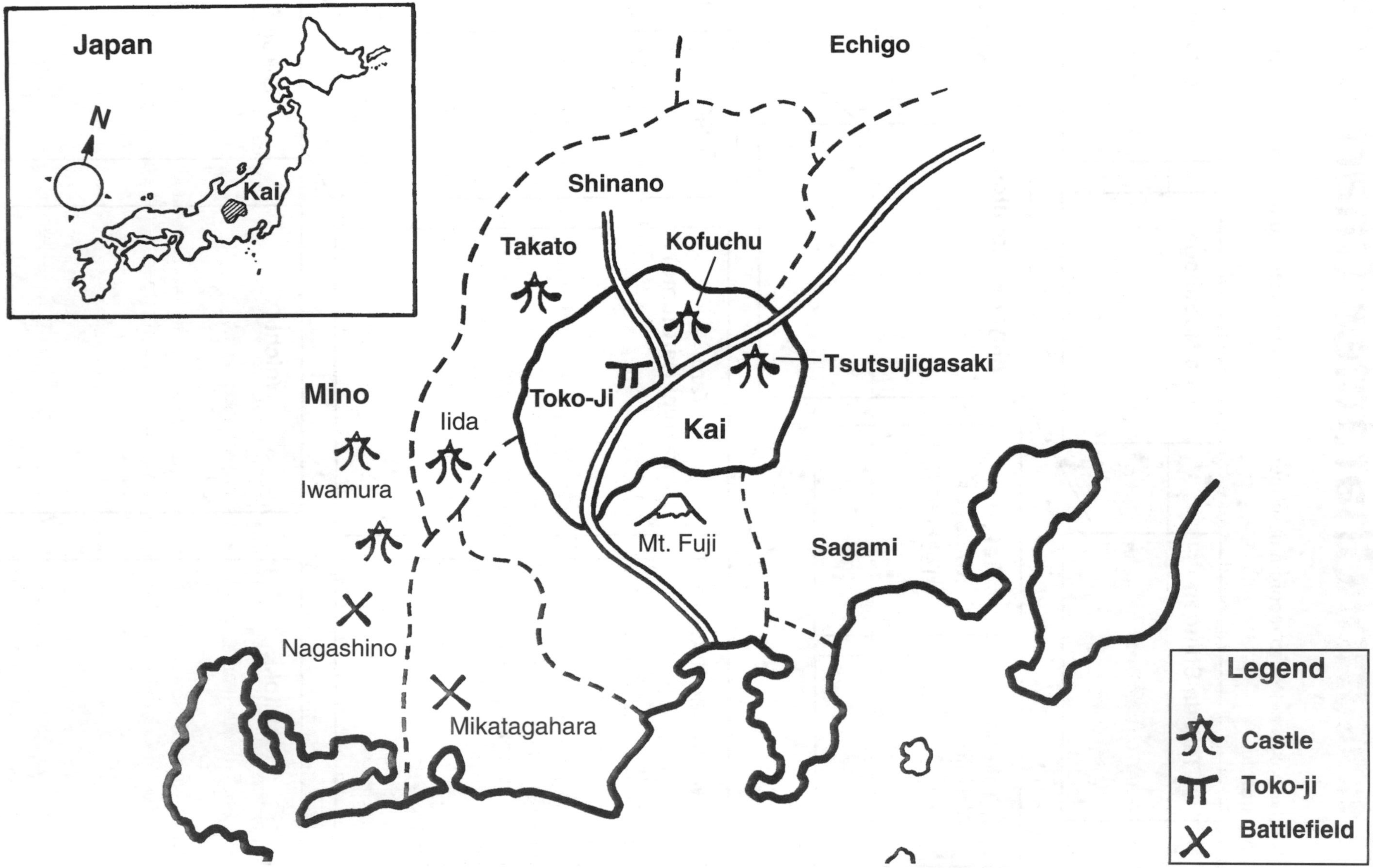

Legend
- Castle
- Toko-ji
- Battlefield

Echigo

Tsutsujigasaki

Sagami

Kofuchu

Shinano

Kai

Mt. Fuji

Toko-Ji

Takato

Mikatagahara

Iida

Mino

Iwamura

Nagashino

Japan

Kai

N

22

Examples of Honor and Loyalty

Make a chart like the one below to place in your journal. As you read be aware of and record examples of behavior that reflect the Japanese concepts of honor, loyalty, and code of proper conduct. After you note the chapter and page number for each example, create an entry in the proper column indicating the character's name and the specific act.

Chapter and Page Numbers	Example of Honor	Example of Loyalty	Example of Code of Conduct

A Stone in the Stream of Your Life

In the beginning of chapter 3, Taro says "In everyone's life there are certain people who have helped to form his character and give a direction to his life; they are like big stones in a river that force the water to alter its course." Many such people are described in Taro's story of becoming a samurai. Think of your life and the people who have helped to shape it in a positive manner. Choose one of these people to write about in an autobiographical composition. Use the outline below to help organize your composition.

Introduction: Use the quote above to introduce the person who has influenced the course of your life in a positive manner. Describe his or her physical appearance, personality, and character traits and tell how you came to know the person.

Body: Describe the event or relationship that influenced your life. Be specific and descriptive as you tell about this influence over time in chronological order.

Conclusion: Describe what the positive influence has meant to you and the course your life has taken. Describe what might be different about you today had this person not come into your life.

Share your composition with the rest of the class if desired. What kinds of people seem to be the most influential over you and your classmates? What people do you feel will have a positive hand at guiding your life in the future? If possible, mail a copy of your composition to the person you wrote about so that person too may know of his/her influence on you.

Time Line of Life

At the opening of chapter 6, Taro states that "Each year that passes is usually remembered by some particular incident that happened during it." Make a time line of your life in which each year is recorded by the most important or memorable event that happened during that year. Interview family members and friends, as well as searching through photo albums to discover an important or memorable event for each year of your life. Present your time line in any visual manner you choose (poster, book, sculpture, collage, chart, etc.) with the date of each year, an important event clearly written, and some kind of picture or drawing for each year. An example is shown below.

Deliver a Message

Imagine you were to run a message across feudal Japan like Taro and Yoshi. What kind of adventures might you encounter? Write a letter to a friend as if you were the messenger for Lord Akiyamo. Describe your journey and any dangers you encountered. Make sure you refer to geographical landmarks, native plants and animals, people, customs, style of dress, and any other information that allows the reader to know you are in fact in 16th century feudal Japan.

Write Your Future

After meeting the old man in the mountains in Chapter 11, Taro and Yoshi discuss the man's ability to read the past and foretell the future. The old man claimed that "In men's hearts their future is written." What do you think the old man meant by this? If you were to search your heart, what do you think is written for your future? Make a time line of your future by completing the phrases below. Describe your life from this day forward until death. What are the necessary steps needed to get from one life event to the next? What things might influence, positively or negatively, your future in school, college, career, family, friends, hobbies, retirement, and death? Share your future time line with others. Does it seem believable or farfetched? Why?

In men's hearts their future is written.

the teen years

in my twenties

in my thirties

forty to sixty-five

retirement

I pass on

Choose a Name

In ancient Japan, children were given names at birth. However, when they became teenagers, they were allowed to choose new names that gave them adult status. Research to discover more about your name and the process your family used to name you. Use a separate sheet of paper to answer the following questions:

1. What is the full name written on your birth certificate?

2. Does your family name (last name) have any meaning or history? For example, many times families were forced to shorten their names or change them so that they are easier to pronounce. Research to find the origins of your family name and what the name means.

3. Does your given name(s) (first and middle names) have any meaning or history? Why did your parents choose this/these name(s) for you?

4. When deciding on names, what other names did your parents consider for you? If you had been a boy instead of a girl or a girl instead of a boy, what might your name have been?

5. Imagine you lived in ancient Japan and were allowed to change your name upon reaching adulthood. What would you name yourself? Give yourself a new first and last name, and if you want, a new middle name as well. Describe why you chose each of these names and the significance they hold for your adult years. Each name must have a meaning and not just be pleasing to you.

The Samurai's Tale

Profound Proverbs

The Japanese used many proverbs to help guide their actions and conduct. Look up each of the following proverbs in the story. On the line write what you think each proverb means.

Chapter 3 *Impoliteness marks you as a fool, for it takes away from you an advantage and gives you none in return.*

_____

Chapter 7 *Pride can take refuge in rags and humbleness as well as in silken robes.*

_____

Chapter 11 *It is best when the vessel and what it contains are both of the same quality.*

_____

Chapter 11 *The butterfly in spring does not know it will die in autumn; intoxicated by its own beauty, it flutters from flower to flower, thinking that its life will last forever.*

_____

Chapter 13 *A loose tongue can outrun a horse.*

_____

Chapter 15 *A man's life is but the evening breeze that rises at sunset and makes the bamboo sway.*

_____

Chapter 16 *The answers of a wise man can make a fool angry, but the questions of a fool should not be able to anger a wise man.*

_____

Chapter 18 *The moon and the stars are constant; it is within ourselves that changes take place, and that is why we admire that lantern in the sky at night.*

_____

Now You Try It

Read the following proverbs or sayings used today. Describe what each saying means, and then change each saying into a Japanese-style proverb. Use a separate piece of paper, if necessary.

1. An apple a day keeps the doctor away. _____

2. Early to bed and early to rise keeps a man healthy, wealthy, and wise. _____

3. The early bird catches the worm. _____

4. Don't count your chickens before they're hatched. _____

An Abundance of Fathers

In chapter 28, Lord Akiyamo claims that Taro has had an abundance of fathers. What does he mean by this remark? Who are the fathers to whom he refers? Make a list of the men in Taro's life and how each of them has acted as a "father" to him. Site specific examples from the book, naming the chapters and page numbers where you found supporting evidence. Use the chart below as a guide.

Name	Evidence of "Fatherly Behavior"	Chapter and Pages
Togan		
Lord Akiyamo		
Wada Kansuke		
Lord Zakoji		
Yoichi		

Write an Epilogue

At the end of the story Murakami Harutomo, Aki-hime, and Yoichi were reunited and returned to Kofuchu. The reader is left with a sense of revenge and a possible sequel to this story with the words of Murakami: "The prayer says that 'in the raging fire of the world, there is no peace.' Yet that is not altogether true, for in the love between two human beings, that fire can be quenched and peace may be found."

What do you think our hero meant by these words? What will happen to the three characters? Will peace be found in Japan? Write an epilogue to this story that answers these questions.

The Sign of the Chrysanthemum

by Katherine Paterson

Summary

Muna's mother dies when he is thirteen. Muna or "No Name" is then left alone with his mother's poverty and a dream to find his father—a samurai he has never known. His mother had told him stories of this great man, whom she had barely known herself. She claimed Muna would know him by the sign of the chrysanthemum on his shoulder. Muna travels to the dangerous and bewildering capital of twelfth-century Japan with high aspirations of claiming his birthright into the noble warrior or samurai class. Befriended, then tricked, by a ronin, Muna eventually finds shelter as a servant to a master swordmaker. Throughout his difficult investigation, Muna struggles with becoming a man himself and humbly making his new way in the world. During the exciting course of the book, the author colorfully describes the culture, history, and lifestyle of the ancient Japanese surviving on the verge of revolution.

This outline is a suggested plan for using the various activities that are presented in this book. Each of the lessons can take from one to several days to complete.

Sample Plan

Lesson 1
- ❏ Introduce students to the history of Japan, page 29.
- ❏ Make a time line, focusing on the twelfth century, pages 44–45.
- ❏ Learn more about the changes in social order, page 47.
- ❏ Create organizational folders, page 77.
- ❏ Review vocabulary activities, page 8.

Lesson 2
- ❏ Read chapters 1–3 of *The Sign of the Chrysanthemum*.
- ❏ Assign a vocabulary activity, page 8.
- ❏ Answer the comprehension questions for this section, page 30.
- ❏ Learn more about death in ancient Japan, page 15.
- ❏ Make a family mon, page 67.
- ❏ Explore Japan's geography by making a map, page 46.

Lesson 3
- ❏ Read chapters 4–6 of *The Sign of the Chrysanthemum*.
- ❏ Assign a vocabulary activity, page 8.
- ❏ Answer the comprehension questions for this section, page 30.
- ❏ Learn more about Japanese festivals, page 52.
- ❏ Experiment with the Zen way of life, pages 12–13.
- ❏ Write a tanka and/or a haiku poem, page 39.
- ❏ Compare the lifestyle of a samurai and a knight, page 48.

Lesson 4
- ❏ Read chapters 7–10 of *The Sign of the Chrysanthemum*.
- ❏ Assign a vocabulary activity, page 8.
- ❏ Answer the comprehension questions for this section, page 31.
- ❏ Discuss ancient social customs, pages 49–51.
- ❏ Compare the Shinto and Buddhist religions, page 14.
- ❏ Write about a time when you were treated unfairly, page 32.
- ❏ Design a medieval Japanese castle, page 64.

Lesson 5
- ❏ Read chapters 11–14 of *The Sign of the Chrysanthemum*.
- ❏ Assign a vocabulary activity, page 8.
- ❏ Answer the comprehension questions for this section, page 31.
- ❏ Write a persuasive composition, page 32.
- ❏ Examine similes and metaphors from the story, page 33.

Lesson 6
- ❏ Read chapters 15–18 of *The Sign of the Chrysanthemum*.
- ❏ Assign a vocabulary activity, page 8.
- ❏ Answer the comprehension questions for this section, page 31.
- ❏ Evaluate other Japanese proverbs, page 41.
- ❏ Choose a new name, page 25.
- ❏ Discuss themes in literature, page 34.
- ❏ Write an epilogue to the story, page 34.
- ❏ Plan a Bunraku puppet show, pages 61–63 , or Noh play, page 69, to review the story plot.
- ❏ Complete one or more of the culminating activities from the unit, pages 70–76.
- ❏ Assign further reading on the subject, page 19.

Overview of Activities

Setting the Stage

1. Introduce students to the age of ancient Japan by following the steps on page 6. Have students further investigate the time period of the book by making a time line (pages 44–45). Draw their focus to the revolutionary times of the 12th century and the unstable government. Help students understand the workings of a feudal society by completing the activity on page 47.

2. Assemble the Japanese bulletin board (page 77) for students to use as the unit progresses. Make organizational folders/journals (page 77) containing copies of the appropriate vocabulary lists (page 30) and comprehension questions (pages 30–31). Review the different vocabulary activities (page 8) and choose one or more of these activities to use throughout the duration of the story.

3. Before reading the book, have students try to imagine what their lives would be like if they were left with no parents, no home, no money, and no material goods. Predict as a class what would most likely happen to such a youth in our day and age. What options would be available today? Would such a youth have much future striking out on his or her own in the world? Tell students that this is what the main character of the story is about to do.

Enjoying the Book

1. Begin reading the first selection in *The Sign of the Chrysanthemum*. Discuss Muna's actions and predict what he might encounter in the next selection. Did Muna make wise decisions? What codes of conduct are controlling his behavior? How has Muna been lucky with the people he has met? What would you have done differently if you had been Muna?

2. Have students complete a vocabulary activity in their journals. Review the comprehension questions for this selection. Just as you would use a variety of strategies to teach the vocabulary, use a variety of strategies to reinforce comprehension—whole class discussions, small group work, individual responses, games, debates, etc.

3. Follow the sample plan to complete other activities as the story progresses. Allow ample time to discuss each reading selection as well as its vocabulary and comprehension questions.

Extending the Book

1. After completing the book, have students discuss and write about the two prevailing themes in the story (page 34). Have groups of students work together to formulate epilogues (page 34) to the story that help explain some unanswered questions from the book.

2. Have groups of students prepare a Bunraku puppet show (pages 61–63) or Noh play (page 69) to reenact different chapters or scenes from the book. Choose one or more of the suggested culminating activities (page 70–76) to finish the study of this book.

3. For further reading on this topic, have students check out other books about ancient Japan written by Katherine Paterson and other authors. Refer to the annotated list on page 19 or the bibliography on page 79 for suggestions.

Vocabulary Lists

Chapters 1–3		Chapters 7–10	Chapters 11–14
serfs	typhoons	artisan	feverish
daimyos	stowaway	brocade	perversely
drudgery	loutish	apprentice	fitful
orphan	eluded	presumptuous	hampered
prostrate	halberds	unctuous	gaggle
ronin		ebullient	treacherous
		incredulously	
Chapters 4–6		menial	**Chapters 15–18**
provinces	irreverent	pique	meticulous
brazier	repented	effusive	15 { hypocrite
Buddha	prominent	bawdy	portico
despise	methodical	garish	arrogant
roguish	epitaph	cadence	brutish
			perfidy

Comprehension Questions

Chapters 1–3

Ch 1
1. Why did Muna feel his mother's death was her release? How did her death also free Muna?
2. What does Muna hope to find with the discovery of his father?

Ch 2 3. Why do you think Takanobu saved Muna on the ship?

Ch 3 4. Why is Muna disappointed at his introduction to Heiankyo—The Capital of Eternal Peace?

5. What actually is Rokujo Avenue? *No -*

Chapters 4–6

1. How might the scene at the Rushomon Gate provide foreshadowing for Muna's future?

2. Why do Takanobu and his friends get Muna a job at the imperial stables? What advantages does
Ch 4   this give the warriors?

3. What evidence is given that Takanobu and his friends are enemies to Lord Kiyomori and the
Heike warriors?

4. Why do you think Takanobu sent Muna to find Plum Face? What does this errand have to do with
the fire?   → *Character sketch of Takanobu - use vocab words*

Ch 5 5. Why does Muna feel fortunate to have been taken in at the sword maker's shop? How might this
help his pursuit?

6. In chapter 6 Fukuji says, "Pride, pride, pride. It will slay us all in the end . . . . Perhaps a man is
never truly destroyed except by his own hand." How might this provide foreshadowing for
Ch 6   Muna's future?

7. Why is Fukuji so choosy about the buyers of his swords?

Comprehension Questions *(cont.)*

Chapters 7–10

Ch 7
1. Learning of Kawaki's great sickness makes Muna aware of the sorrows of the world, yet this does not make him unhappy. Why?

2. Why is Muna so hesitant to tell Fukuji his plan? What does this tell you about Japanese customs and pride?

Ch 8
3. Why do you think Takanobu is disguised as a monk? What does he want from Muna?

4. Why does Muna not ask to see the chrysanthemum tattoo when Takanobu claims to be his father? Do you think the tattoo would have been there? Why or why not?

Ch 9
5. Muna claims that "The luckless must snatch their own luck." What does this tell you about Muna's future plans?

Ch 10 —
6. What happens to Akiko after her father dies? Why does this not seem terrible to her uncle?

Chapters 11–14

Ch 11
1. Muna claims, "I will use them as they have used me." To whom is he referring? Do you feel Muna has been used by everyone he has met? Explain your reasoning.

Ch 12 — 2. What does Muna hope to gain by stealing the sword for Takanobu? How is he disappointed?

Ch 14
3. Why does Takanobu visit Fukuji?

4. Do you think Takanobu is really Muna's father? Why or why not?

Chapters 15–18

Ch 15
1. Why does Fukuji set out to see Lord Kiyomori when they are not on good terms? What does this tell you about Fukuji's feelings toward Muna?

2. Why does Lord Kiyomori's background make him more sympathetic to Muna's situation?

3. Why is Fukuji considered a hypocrite?

4. Why does Fukuji not continue to search for Muna?

Ch 16 5. Earlier in the book, Fukuji claimed that pride would slay them in the end. How has Muna destroyed himself with his own pride?

17 6. Why do you think Muna took the sword back to Fukuji?

7. What do you think happened to Takanobu when the fighting began? *Why?*

8. Why does Muna choose to keep his name?

9. What message(s) do you think the author has tried to convey throughout the story?

final questions – Throughout the story many references were made about Japanese culture + customs. Describe three + (two) tell why they are an important aspect of Japanese life.

35 questions, 2.57
+ final

Treated as a Child

In chapter 9, Muna proposes that he join Fukuji as an apprentice. When he does not receive the response he desires, he feels that he has been treated as a child. What would you have done if you were Muna? Would you have told Fukuji that you were not a child and then proved your words?

Think of a time in your life when you felt that you were unfairly treated as a child. It may have been the rules at home, responsibilities in school, or some other situation in the recent past that made you feel this way. Write an autobiographical account of the incident, telling what happened, what you did, and how it made you feel. Use the outline below to organize your composition.

Introduction: Describe what happened to Muna and how you feel you were once treated unfairly as a child.

Body: Describe the situation in chronological order. Make sure you include appropriate dialogue and descriptions of the people involved. Describe your feelings about the situation and what you did about it.

Conclusion: Describe what you have learned from this situation and how it has changed, or not changed, the way you are treated. If you could do it over again, would you react differently? Why or why not?

Share your composition with the rest of the class if desired. Discuss how your situations are similar or different. How does the phrase "At what age comes responsibility?" dictate how you are viewed and treated? What would you do in the future to be treated more as an adult and less as a child?

Is He the Father?

In chapter 14, Takanobu confronts Fukuji, claiming to be Muna's real father. Given the evidence from the story so far, do you think he is the father? Write a persuasive composition supporting your beliefs. Make sure you cite supporting evidence from the book and the chapters in which you found the evidence. Use the outline below to help organize your composition.

Introduction: Give some background information about Muna's search for his father. Tell whether or not you believe Takanobu to be this father, and list three reasons for your argument.

Body: State your first reason and describe the supporting evidence from the book.

State your second reason and describe the supporting evidence from the book.

State your third reason and describe the supporting evidence from the book.

Conclusion: Summarize your points, and again state whether or not you believe Takanobu is Muna's real father.

Share compositions as a class to determine what the majority believes. If desired, hold a class debate to further investigate this persuasive argument.

Similes and Metaphors

A **simile** is a figure of speech in which one thing is likened to a dissimilar thing using *like* or *as*. *Example:* The sword reflected the sunlight like a calm Shinto pond on a clear morning.

A **metaphor** is a figure of speech in which one thing is likened to a different thing by being spoken of as if it were that other. *Example:* The sword was a cool Shinto pond reflecting the winter morning's sunlight.

Throughout the story, Katherine Paterson uses a variety of figurative language to engage her reader and paint a mental picture of the people and places in ancient Japan. Review the following similes and metaphors used in the text. Decide whether each phrase is considered a simile or a metaphor. Then explain what each line was describing and what it means.

Chapter 1 . . . *like a great, lazy cat stretched out for a summer nap.*

_____

Chapter 2 . . . *moved in two antlike lines up and down the gangplank.*

_____

Chapter 4 . . . *for the insatiable dragon had already engorged the flimsy wooden structure and had gone on, belching flames, to satisfy its appetite elsewhere.*

_____

Chapter 9 . . . *like an animal caught between two opposing lines of bowmen—all of the arrows flying toward him.*

_____

Chapter 9 *The silence rose and grew like the approach of a tidal wave.*

_____

Now You Try It

Use both similes and metaphors to describe each of the people and situations below. Be as descriptive and elaborate as possible.

1. Muna as he planned to steal the sword _____

_____

2. Takanobu as he reacted to Muna's proposition of fatherhood_____

_____

3. The hike up the hill to the shrine_____

_____

4. The old man on the hill _____

_____

Themes in Literature

Throughout most stories the author tries to convey a message or theme to the reader. Read the following two statements from the book. Describe how these two statements provide a message or theme for the story.

Blesses as well the lowly and the small.

Through fire is the spirit forged.

Write an Epilogue

Imagine there was one more chapter to the book. What would it be about? What do you think is in Muna's future? Write an epilogue to this story in which the following questions are answered:

1. What happens to Muna now that he is a swordmaker's apprentice?

2. Does Muna continue to search for his father? Why or why not?

3. What ever happened to Takanobu? How did Muna find out?

4. What becomes of Akiko? Does Muna ever go back to save her, or does he learn to forget about her?

Share your epilogue with the rest of the class. Is your prediction similar to or different from those of your classmates?

Influencing Muna

Throughout the story, Muna was influenced by four main characters in both positive and negative ways. List the four main characters on a sheet of writing paper and describe how they influenced Muna and the decisions he made. Give examples from the book with chapters and page numbers.

Name	How they have influenced Muna's life	Chapters and Page Numbers
Takanobu		
Akiko		
Kawaki		
Fukuji		

Influence on our lives can come from unexpected people at unexpected moments. Think of times in your life when someone influenced your behavior and attitude with a comment or action. Describe the situation and how this person influenced your behavior, be it in a positive or negative manner. How has that influence affected the rest of your life? If you could tell this person today how they influenced you, what would you say? If possible, write a letter to this person describing the effect they have had on you.

Letter to a Friend

Imagine you are a youth in ancient Japan and your parents have just successfully arranged your marriage and planned for your living arrangements. Write a letter to a friend describing the upcoming event, your feelings, and what life is like in a family in ancient Japan. Use the proper friendly letter format and the outline below to help organize your letter.

Introduction: Explain why you are writing. Tell the news about your upcoming marriage and give background about arranged-marriage customs. Describe the duties of the head of the family and his responsibilities to the family. Describe your duties as the child.

Body: Describe your intended marriage partner and what little you know about him/her. Describe your new house or the house and occupants where you will be living. Describe the engagement party, the food served, and the clothes you and your intended wore.

Closing: Describe your feelings about this arranged marriage and why you feel this way. Close with a short poem or verse and ask your friend to respond.

Discuss the class letters and how things are different today. How do students of today feel about arranged marriages? Why? What benefits are there to choosing your own marriage partner? What benefits are there to having an arranged marriage?

Kyoto Courtiers and Peasants

During the Heiann Period in ancient Japan, culture flourished in the capital of Kyoto under the regal influence of the Fujiwara clan. Although only five percent of Kyoto societies were courtiers, or people who took part in the highly refined social life of the court, their influence spanned the ages. Write two diary entries describing this time period from two different perspectives.

1. Imagine you are a Kyoto courtier in 1100. A.D. Write a diary describing your week. Include information about food, clothing, your living quarters, art, literature, poetry, and religion. Describe your "work" or activities that fill your days. Then describe your feelings about the "others"—people in society that do not share your noble lifestyle. Why do you feel it is fair to live in such luxury while others in your province are poor and starving?

2. Now imagine you are a poor Kyoto peasant in A.D. 1100 who labors on a noble estate and lives in a crowded hut. Write a diary describing your week. Include information about your food, clothing, living quarters, and what you do for fun. Describe your work and how you spend your day. Then describe your feelings toward the courtiers in Kyoto and your lowly social position. Do you accept your fate, or do you feel it is unjust?

Share and discuss these different perspectives as a class. Why did the peasant class not fight for more rights? Why did feudalism continue longer in Japan than in Europe? What cultural influences maintained this system?

Japanese Fairy Tales

Like all other cultures around the world, Japan developed stories and tales to help pass on the cultural values, hopes, and dreams of its people. The following story is one of its most popular:

The Bamboo-Cutter's Tale

Once upon a time, deep in a bamboo forest, there lived an old man and his wife. The forest was a beautiful place to live, with its timid creatures, grassy knolls, and thick bamboo stalks. However, life was rather dreary and lonely for the old couple for they were very poor and had no children of their own to love and care for. The old man spent long days outdoors cutting the tall stalks of a bamboo. He used the bamboo to make hats, baskets, tableware, and other goods that he sold to the city folk. No one knew his real name. Everyone simply called him "the bamboo-cutter," and this is his wondrous tale.

One morning the old man walked through the forest, searching for a straight bamboo to cut. Just as he entered the darkest part of a thicket, he spied a golden halo of light streaming from a single, slender bamboo plant. The old man was astonished, for never before had he seen such a sight in all his years in the forest. Summoning his courage, he took out his axe and felled the stalk with one swift stroke. Suddenly, the halo of light vanished, and out from the hollow stem tumbled a tiny baby girl. She was only about three inches high, but she was the cutest thing the old man had ever seen. He lifted the wee girl gently into the palm of his hand and carefully carried her back to his house.

Upon reaching his home the old man burst inside the room and called for his wife. Together they examined the precious little bundle. Based on the story of her miraculous discovery, they decided that she must have been a gift from the gods and named her Kaguya-hime, which means "Radiant Princess." The old couple proved to be worthy parents, doting on their little girl and showering her with love. To add to their joy, almost every day the old man would come across a glowing bamboo in the thicket. Instead of a baby, out dropped piles of gold coins! Before long the old couple were very, very wealthy, and this allowed them to raise Kaguya-hime in a manner befitting a true princess.

Of course Kaguya-hime proved to be no ordinary baby girl either. She grew astonishingly fast, sometimes as much as an inch in a single day, and each day she also grew more radiant and full of life. The old man often thought, "There's nothing I wouldn't do for that little girl!" Kaguya-hime didn't remain a little girl for very long. In just three short months, she had grown into a mature young maiden, so beautiful that anyone who looked upon her fell hopelessly in love.

Japanese Fairy Tales *(cont.)*

The Bamboo-Cutter's Tale *(cont.)*

Word of the bamboo-cutter's extraordinary daughter quickly spread throughout the land. Soon noblemen were flocking to their home asking for her hand in marriage. Kaguya-hime refused to see them, and her parents turned them away. "I shall never marry," she told the old man and woman, "I will never willingly leave your side." Secretly, the old man was gladdened by her refusals, for he loved his child and dreaded the thought of ever losing her. However, five of the young suitors were not so easily rebuffed. They were men of exceptional wealth, standing, and perseverance who camped outside the door day and night, pleading for a chance to see the beautiful maiden.

The old man was at a loss as to how to discourage these earnest young noblemen, and as time went by he began to feel sorry for them. Finally, he approached his daughter and begged her to choose one as her husband. Kaguya-hime could see her father's torn heart and therefore devised a plan. She assigned five impossible tasks to the suitors and claimed she would marry the one who completed his task. Each young man vowed to return victorious and soon was on his way. Hearing the extent of the tasks, the old man was sure each man would eventually abandon all hope of marrying Kaguya-hime. Imagine his surprise when, months later, all five returned! As each man approached the fair maiden with evidence of his task, Kaguya-hime pronounced it fake and worthless. Mesmerized by her beauty, the suitors agreed with her verdict and left the house dejected and heartbroken, never to see their beloved princess again.

Relieved that the matter was finally settled, life returned to normal in the forest. However, the old man's happiness was short lived, for in the eighth month of the year Kaguya-hime began to change. Night after night she would sit and gaze at the moon as it grew fuller in the sky. As the moon shone brighter and brighter, Kaguya-hime grew more wistful and melancholy. Perplexed by the change in their daughter, the old man and woman softly pried Kaguya-hime for answers. Finally one night the young maiden burst into tears. "Oh, how I wish I could stay with you forever!" she sobbed, "But tomorrow I must return." Her parents gasped at these words and pleaded with their daughter to explain.

Kaguya-hime told them of her real home, the place in which she was born, called the city of the moon. Now that she was grown, the moon people would be coming for her to fulfill her destiny in the sky. With this sad news the three loved ones wrapped their arms around each other and cried. By morning, the old man grew fierce and determined, "We'll never let you go, Kaguya-hime, never!" He thundered from the house and set off to hire a thousand strong samurai to hold the moon people at bay. Standing shoulder to shoulder, the warriors encircled the house. Another contingent guarded the roof with arrows pointed to the sky, while the three family members huddled in the innermost room of the house.

Japanese Fairy Tales *(cont.)*

The Bamboo-Cutter's Tale *(cont.)*

Slowly the moon rose, casting a brilliant halo around the stolid samurai. The arrows that the valiant warriors shot at the light seemed to vanish in midair. The moonbeams pierced the warriors' armor, paralyzing them where they stood. With a flash from that unearthly light, two moon maidens descended with a winged horse and chariot. Magically, the door to the inner room slid open and Kaguya-hime arose and walked outside, as if drawn by some invisible force. The old man and woman now realized there was nothing more they could do. "Kaguya-hime!" they cried, running after their precious daughter, "Take us with you!"

Kaguya-hime turned to face her parents. Her look of sorrow told them there was no possibility of following. Carefully she placed a pouch into their hands. "You have no idea how much I will miss you. Please take this as a token of my gratitude and love. With this medicine you will stay forever young and healthy. Good-bye!" With these words she stepped into the silver chariot. The winged horse shook his mane, and off into the night she disappeared.

With tears streaming down their faces the old couple built a small fire and sat to watch the night sky. The old man passed the small pouch between his two hands, weighing the possibilities. "With this medicine we can live forever." He sighed, gazing first at his beloved wife and then up at the bright full moon. "But, without you Kaguya-hime, how could we ever be happy again?" The old couple smiled at each other and nodded in agreement. "What good is life without happiness?" And with that, the bamboo-cutter tossed the pouch into the fire.

Questions and Activities

1. What does this story tell you about family values, hopes, and dreams in ancient Japan? What do you think is the message the author is trying to convey?

2. What aspects of this story make it a fairy tale?

3. Break the class into small groups and divide the story into scenes. Have each group rewrite and illustrate their scene, adding in more details and figurative language. Combine the scenes to form a class book.

4. Write your own Japanese fairy tale based on one of your favorite classic fairy tales. Change the characters, setting, and plot to make it appear Japanese. Use references to ancient landmarks, customs, clothing, religion, and values of respect and loyalty. Illustrate your fairy tale and share it with others in the class. What message does your fairy tale convey?

Tanka and Haiku Poetry

The ancient Japanese are well known for their poetry. Learning to write poetry was a basic part of one's education, much like learning to read, write, or compute mathematics. The two most popular forms of Japanese poetry are the tanka, which was made popular during the Heian period, and the haiku, which replaced the tanka during the Tokugawa period. Both of these forms create a blend of simplicity and subtlety and can be found in any current literature about ancient Japan.

Tanka

5 lines with a set pattern of syllables

The sun sets at dusk,	*5 syllables*
Deep into the blue abyss	*7 syllables*
Where sea and sky meet	*5 syllables*
To kiss good night to daytime	*7 syllables*
And sleep ever quietly.	*7 syllables*

Haiku

3 lines with a set pattern of syllables

The sun sleeps at dusk,	*5 syllables*
Quietly sinking below	*7 syllables*
A blanket of sea.	*5 syllables*

Now You Try It

Think of a scene or event from your life. Follow the syllable pattern to write a tanka or haiku poem about this scene that describes the setting, your feelings, or the action that took place. Make a final draft of your poem on a special piece of paper, using your best handwriting. If desired, add a simple illustration to accompany your poem.

Extension

In ancient times, people corresponded with poems that told their feelings about life, love, military strategies, and upcoming events. Write a poem to a friend about something that is on your mind. Have your friend answer your poem with a poem of his or her own. The poems can be specific and clear or use abstract metaphors to convey their meaning._____

_____

_____

_____

Westernizing an Isolated Japan

The shoguns successfully defended Japan against invasion by the Mongols in the late thirteenth century. One unwelcome result of this defense was fierce internal fighting, that resulted in two imperial courts and conflicts among warlords.

In the middle of the 16th century, guns and cannons replaced the traditional swords used in warfare in Japan. Under Oda Nobunaga and his successor, Toyotomi Hideyoshi, Japan was unified. Although Tokugawa Ieyasu had pledged to support Toyotomi's son, Hideyori, as shogun, he claimed the title for himself instead. From 1603 to 1868 Japan was ruled by shoguns from the Tokugawa clan. Under their strong leadership, there was peace in Japan, but it was not obtained easily. The Tokugawas ruled by maintaining very strict laws and by dividing the people into defined classes with specific rules about clothing, food, and daily conduct.

To further maintain control, they decided to shut Japan off from foreign influences that might threaten their power. In 1637 all foreigners were thrown out of Japan. Japanese citizens were forbidden to go to other countries, and those living in other countries were forbidden to return home. For more than two hundred years Japan was closed to the outside world.

In 1854 Commodore Matthew Perry of the United States anchored his battleship off the coast and asked Japan to open its doors to the world. Outgunned, the shogun was forced to comply, and soon Japan was trading with outsiders. The Tokugawa shoguns lost power in 1867, and the emperor again ruled Japan. Emperor Meiji realized that if Japan did not become a modern country, it might be conquered by one of the world's stronger nations. He saw to it that railroads and communication systems were brought to Japan. He took away the samurai's power, created a constitution, built a modern army and navy, and started the public school system. In just fifty years, Japan became a modern nation.

What Do You Think?

Do you think it was beneficial for the Tokugawa shoguns to close Japan off from the rest of the world, or do you feel it was damaging?

Write a persuasive composition describing your point of view on the effects of isolating Japan. Use the directions below to help organize your composition.

1. Try to imagine how Japan might be different today if it had always had foreign influence. Make a list of both positive and negative effects on culture, art, government, education, and technology, as well as personal beliefs and behavior.

2. Decide your position on the issue, and then use the outline below to organize your composition.

Introduction: Inform the reader about the isolation of Japan. Tell your position on the issue and list at least three reasons for your position.

Body: Describe each of your reasons in more detail with specific supporting evidence.

Conclusion: Summarize your three reasons again and end with a strong closing statement.

3. Use the writing process to form your composition and then share your argument with the rest of the class and compare the different viewpoints. If desired, hold a class debate on the issue.

Evaluating Japanese Proverbs

Match these Japanese proverbs to their meanings.

Japanese Proverbs

1. _____ Although the owl has large eyes, he can't see as well as a mouse.

2. _____ The cherry tree is known among others by its flowers.

3. _____ Ice coming from water is colder than water.

4. _____ Boat-swallowing fish do not live in brooks.

5. _____ A protruding stake will be hammered in.

6. _____ Although shrimps may dance around, they do not leave the river.

7. _____ Unless you enter the tiger's den, you cannot take the cubs.

8. _____ A cornered rat will bite a cat.

9. _____ Great trees are envied by the wind.

10. _____ Fish do not live in clear water.

11. _____ Though the wind blows, the mountain does not move.

12. _____ Everywhere the crows are black.

Meanings

A. Prominent men in business, politics, and intellectual life are often attacked by lesser men.

B. Be self-disciplined so that you are indifferent to any tumult or disturbance.

C. A talented person stands out among his fellows.

D. A man should not leave his own special occupation, but work according to his own specified position in life.

E. Cramped circumstances do not produce great men.

F. Size does not necessarily denote efficiency.

G. Even the weak when at bay may defeat the strong.

H. Nothing ventured, nothing gained.

I. A son might surpass his parent, master, or teacher in skill.

J. All men everywhere have the same principles in the conduct of life, so we must always act honorably towards all mankind.

K. Deceit and dishonesty are a necessary part of the environment of people who wish to succeed in the world.

L. It is wiser at times to lie low than to be forward, for the latter will certainly cause trouble.

Writing Japanese

Learning to read and write Japanese takes a great deal of time and effort. There are three different kinds of symbols in the language. The first kind are *kanji*, Chinese symbols which were brought to Japan in the fifth century and adapted to the Japanese language. These symbols are used to express ideas. Some kanji are very complicated, requiring several brush strokes that must be written in the correct order and direction. There are over 2,000 kanji in everyday use. Educated Japanese know about 5,000 to 10,000 kanji.

Hiragana and *katakana* are symbols that stand for syllables, not single letters. They are used to spell out words that cannot be written with kanji. Both hiragana and katakana have 48 symbols each. By the time an average Japanese student finishes high school, he or she must know how to read and write 1,850 kanji plus the 48 hiragana and 48 katakana. Even though it is difficult to learn the Japanese language, 99 percent of the Japanese can read and write.

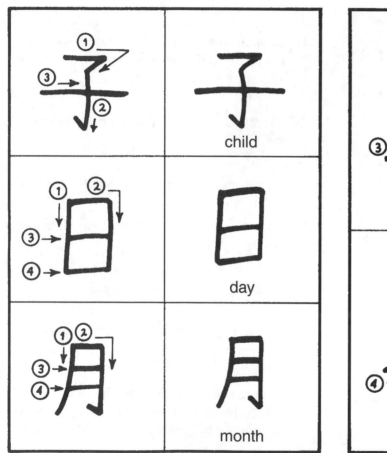

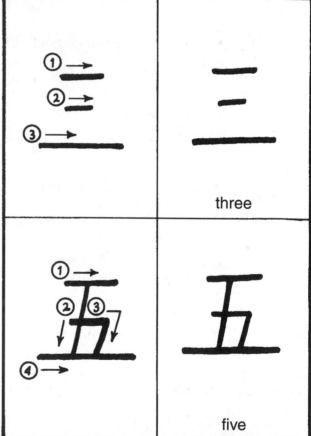

Try Writing These Words in Japanese

Extension: The Japanese write March by placing the "three" over "month." May is written with "five" over "month." Write these months in Japanese.

Creating Japan

Long before the dawn of man there was chaos in the universe. Then Heaven and Earth divided, and the gods came to life. After seven generations had passed, a brother and sister god looked down from the Floating Bridge of Heaven and devised a plan. "The Earth is covered with water far and wide," Izanagi told his sister. "This is not a suitable place for life to grow."

Izanami agreed, "Perhaps we could create a land below and set it to drift upon the ocean. This land would be the beginning of wonderful things!"

So Izanagi thrust his jeweled spear into the ocean. The saltwater that dropped from the sky as he withdrew his sword became the islands of Japan, the first land on earth. Soon Izanagi and Izanami created other gods and goddesses who struggled for power. When his wife died giving birth to the fire god, Izanagi went to the underworld to retrieve her. She refused to come back with him, and they parted forever.

When Izanagi returned from the underworld, he performed the first cleansing ritual. He washed his left eye and created the sun goddess Amaterasu. When he washed his right eye, the moon goddess Tsuki-Yumi came forth. From his nose he created Susanowo, the god of the seas and the storms. When Amaterasu was chosen as the ruler of the Plain of High Heaven, Susanowo ruined her rice fields and threw a dead horse into her palace. Amaterasu became so angry that she hid in a cave and refused to come out. Without her, the world went dark.

Hoping to coax her out, the other gods and goddesses sent a mirror, a crowing rooster, and singing birds to the cave. They laughed and danced so loudly that soon Amaterasu grew curious. Finally, she peered out, extending her rays. When she emerged, a strong god grabbed her and held her while others sealed off the cave. Unable to retreat back into hiding, Amaterasu told the other gods and goddesses about Susanowo's mischief. The gods and goddesses banished Susanowo to earth, and his descendants lived on the Japanese islands.

Many years later Amaterasu sent her grandson, Ninigi, down to Japan to take control of Honshu Island. He brought with him a magic mirror, a sword, and jewels to prove his divine status and right to rule Japan. After two generations of conflict, Ninigi's grandson, Jimmu Tenno, finally conquered the storm god's people to become the first human emperor of Japan. Since his reign in 660 B.C., there have been 125 emperors in Japan, all descended from Jimmu, the longest unbroken line of emperors in the world.

Many beliefs in Japan's culture are related to this creation story. Although these beliefs are difficult for outsiders to understand, the story above gives some important insights into some traditional Japanese beliefs. For example, the emperors of Japan claim to be direct descendants of the gods, not merely human beings. Emperors were revered and worshipped as gods. Many people in Japan also consider themselves superior to other humans around the earth because they are descended from and chosen by the gods as the leading race of people. The sun goddess Amaterasu is still worshipped today at the Ise Shrine on Honshu Island. Even the name for Japan is related to this goddess, for Japan in Japanese is Nippon or the Land of the Rising Sun.

Discussion, Research, and Activities

1. How is this creation story similar to or different from other creation stories around the world? Research other stories from the Bible, Native American folklore, Egypt, Greece, and China.

2. Japan has many names—The Land of the Rising Sun, The Land of Fresh Rice, Ears of a Thousand Autumns, and The Land of Abundant Reed Plains. What would be some good names for your country? Why?

Period Time Line

1. Cut out the three time line strips on pages 44 and 45 and tape them together in chronological order.

2. Draw a picture in each box that corresponds with the events, people, or achievements of that period. Write the description of each period on the back of the boxes.

3. Color your period time line and hang it with yarn.

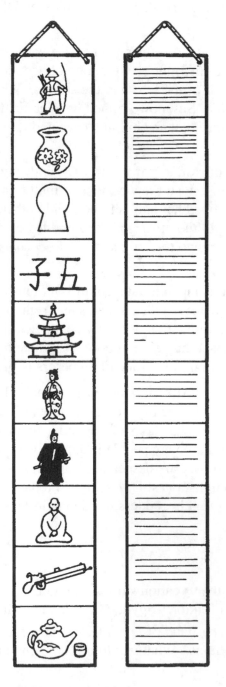

Prehistoric Japan

Jomon Period, 8000 B.C.–300 B.C.

Yayoi Period, 300 B.C.–A.D. 300

Tomb Culture Period, A.D. 300–A.D. 500

Period Time Line *(cont.)*

Classical Japan

Early Historic Period, A.D. 500–A.D. 710

Nara Period, A.D. 710–A.D. 794.

Heian Period, A.D. 794.–A.D. 1185

Medieval Japan

Kamakura Period, A.D. 1185–A.D. 1333

Ashikaga Period, A.D. 1333–A.D. 1573

Period of Unification, A.D. 1573.–A.D. 1600

Tokugawa Period, A.D. 1600.–A.D. 1867

Mapping the Land

Label and color the map below, using an atlas and the following directions:

1. Label and color the four major islands: Hokkaido—red, Honshu—orange, Shikoku—yellow, and Kyushu—green.

2. Label the major waterways and color them blue: Pacific Ocean, Sea of Okhotsk, Tsugara Strait, Sea of Japan, Korea Strait, Ise Bay.

3. Mark the locations of the following cities with a dot and label: Edo (Tokyo), Ise, Osaka, Kobe, Heian (Kyoto), Nara, Nagasaki.

4. Mark the location of Mount Fuji with a triangle and label.

5. Label the following countries on the inset map: Russia, Manchuria, China, Korea.

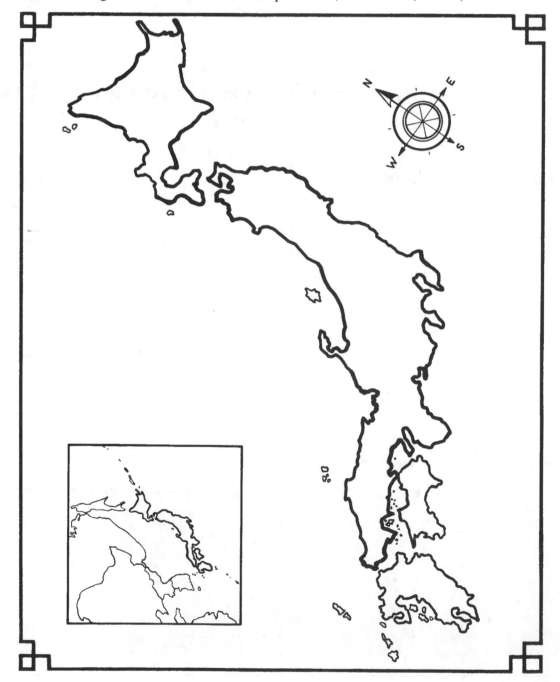

Ancient Social Customs

The Japanese people are a blend of early settlers from Northern Japan and immigrants from mainland Asia and islands in the Pacific. Because they were isolated from other countries for centuries, the Japanese almost never mixed with non-Japanese. They all speak the same language and share many customs, values, and beliefs. Their common background and language help keep harmony within the population.

Many of these customs and behaviors can be traced to ancient times and the blending of religious traditions. The ancient religion of Shinto emphasizes harmony with nature and honoring ancestors and family. In ancient times and today, each family is held responsible for the behavior of its members both socially and legally. This belief also extends to other groups such as school, work, community, and country. If the group does well, everyone feels good. If one member of the group does something wrong, it reflects badly on the entire group. The group, more than the individual, is considered very important, and everyone in the group must get along.

Buddhism is another religion that has influenced Japanese social customs and behavior. During the reign of the samurai class, Zen Buddhism spread throughout the culture. Zen stresses self-discipline as a way of balancing the mind, body, and spirit. One way the Japanese practice self-discipline is by being polite and showing respect. They will hide their own feelings rather than hurt someone else's, and they will not speak back to a person of higher position regardless of the situation. Bowing is another way to show manners and respect. The one who bows lowest, longest, and the most times is always the person with a lower rank or position.

The philosophies of Confucius also influenced the Japanese way of life and strengthened the concepts of respect for obedience, loyalty, and clearly defined rules. This system of thought and belief came to Japan from China and Korea in the fifth century. Confucianism stresses the importance of right behavior and fulfilling one's duty to those higher on the social ladder. This was especially true in ancient times when laws reflected different rights and consequences for those of different social positions.

As in ancient times, there are rules today for how to do just about everything in Japan—how to wrap presents, use chopsticks, pour tea, eat noodles, arrange flowers, etc. Although most rules are the same for all people, some rules differ depending upon your social rank. Today people are ranked according to age, sex, and social status. Older people rank higher than younger people, and men rank higher than women. Three minority groups are considered to have a lower social status than the rest of the Japanese. The largest minority group is called *burakumin*, or outcasts. These are people who hold jobs, or whose ancestors held jobs, involving blood and death. People who work in butchering animals or any aspects of funerals are considered burakumin. People of Korean descent and the native Ainu people are also considered lower than other Japanese. Understanding this blend of ancient religions and philosophies helps us to understand the customs and behavior of the Japanese today. Although we may not agree with some of their social customs, it is important to respect the beliefs of others around the world.

Ancient Social Customs *(cont.)*

Choose one or more of the following activities for research, discussion, or debate to explore the social customs of ancient Japan and how they compare to our own.

Family Responsibility: In Japan, the family is held responsible for the behavior of its members. This means that the parents are responsible for the actions of their children both socially and legally.

1. How do you think this influences the way that the Japanese raise their children? How do you think this influences their justice system? How do you think this influences the way couples view marriage and divorce, having a family, and working with other members of their extended family?

2. Describe both the pros and cons of this belief system in which the family is responsible for all of its members. What aspects of this belief system do you feel would enhance our country and the responsibility of family?

Group Versus the Individual: In order to get along and be successful, the importance of the group, rather than the individual, is stressed in Japan. This can be seen in many ways, such as Japanese companies and business dealings and the loyalty of kamikaze pilots in World War II.

1. Research other ways the Japanese put the group ahead of the individual.

2. Think of situations in our country in which the success of the entire group is considered more important than the rights of an individual—actions of the president, war, sports teams, businesses, etc. Why might making decisions based on the success of the entire group rather than a few individuals be important in certain situations? How might acting on your own individual behalf be detrimental to some of these situations?

3. There are many examples throughout history in which individuals defended themselves by claiming to be acting on orders for the good of the group rather than thinking or acting for themselves. Such cases include the Nazis in Germany, those who dropped the atomic bomb at Hiroshima, and Oliver North at the Iran/Contra hearings. Research these and other similar cases. Do you feel the individual should be held responsible for his or her actions? At what point should an individual disobey orders given for the good of the group because it goes against his or her individual beliefs?

4. List some of the different groups to which you belong (family, class at school, sports team, church youth group, club, scouts, etc.). In each of these groups which is more important, the individual or the whole group? In each of these groups can you behave however you want, or do you need to consider the feelings and success of the entire group when you act? Are there times in which the group is more important and other times in which the individual is more important? How do you feel rules help to keep a balance between the two?

Being Polite: The rules for manners and proper conduct are highly regarded by the Japanese. Because of these rules they do not always act the way that they feel. This makes communication between our cultures very difficult since they may say one thing while meaning another.

1. When is it good to hide your true feelings, and when is it bad? List some situations in which you might be tempted to lie to be polite and not hurt someone's feelings. Does being honest always mean saying exactly what you feel? As a class discuss some constructive ways to express your feelings without lying while respecting the feelings of others.

2. The Japanese do not question authority since it would show disrespect. Do you feel there are times when you should question authority? List these situations.

Ancient Social Customs *(cont.)*

3. Do you feel there is a right and wrong way to question authority and protest? Research different styles of protest through history—some are violent while others are non-violent. Which of these forms do you feel were most successful? Why do you think they were able to change the thinking and actions of others?

4. Sometimes you are faced with a situation with which you do not agree. You have a choice to obey without question or to speak your mind. What do you feel would be the proper way to question or to protest against a decision made by your teacher or principal at school? What about a rule made by your parents?

5. In our culture the rules of manners and etiquette have changed over time. Research etiquette of the past and compare our behavior today to that described in the past. Are there any rules that you feel should be re-established in order to get along better with each other? What rules of conduct are considered outdated and foolish due to changes in communication, technology, and fashion?

Beliefs in Social Status:

1. How is the treatment of the Ainu people of Japan similar to the treatment of Native Americans in our society in terms of land, occupations, income, and living conditions? Do you feel the Native Americans are considered in a lower class than the rest of the population? Why or why not? What could we do to ensure equality for all of the people in the nation?

2. Review the creation story of Japan. How do you think the belief in this story affects the Japanese outlook on social rank? How do you think it affects the Japanese outlook on all people who are not Japanese?

3. The Japanese treat the old with more respect than the young. Do you feel this is right? How are the elderly treated in our nation?

4. As in some other countries around the world, men are considered to have a higher rank than women in Japan. This was also once true in America. Research ways in which women gained more rights and respect in history. Do you think things will also change in Japan? Why or why not?

5. How do we rank society? How do we show respect for those of higher rank? Many people say children no longer have respect for adults. Do you think this is true? Why or why not? Do you think we as a nation need to increase our use of manners and respect towards others? Similarly, who do you feel deserves more status and respect in our society? Why?

Japanese Festivals

Like all cultures around the world, the Japanese like to celebrate special occasions with festivals. The highest festival of the year is O-shogatsu, or New Year's. People prepare for the holiday by cleaning their houses and paying off their debts so that they can have a fresh start for the coming year. They decorate their homes and streets with a variety of natural materials—pine branches to represent strength and long life, bamboo stalks to represent strong character, and straw rope for good luck and expelling evil spirits. New Year's cards are also sent, and all arrive on New Year's Day!

People worship at the many temples and shrines on New Year's Eve. At midnight, temple bells ring 108 times to signal the beginning of the New Year. The next day families put on their best clothes to visit the homes of relatives and friends. They take with them red envelopes filled with money for the children and small gifts, including chrysanthemum flowers, for the adults. Some of the older people enjoy playing an ancient card game called Songs of a Hundred Poets, in which they match the first and last lines of famous poems.

Another major holiday in Japan is celebrated by Japanese girls on the third of March. The Doll's Festival is a time for girls to share their doll collections, eat special rice cakes, and sing songs. Special displays are made with 15 dolls in ancient costumes placed on stands covered with red cloth and peach blossoms. The peach flower is special for girls, representing gentleness and happiness in marriage. The 15 dolls represent the emperor and empress, court ladies, and musicians. The displays can range from simple to elaborate and may include intricate designs with miniature furniture and food.

Boys, too, have their own holiday. On May 5th, families fly colorful paper carps from bamboo poles outside their homes. The carp is considered brave and strong, and parents hope their children will grow up as determined as this sacred fish. Flying kites and displaying irises are other ways this holiday is celebrated.

All children enjoy another festival called *Shichi-go-san*, or Seven–Five–Three Day. Long ago people believed that the numbers three, five, and seven were unlucky. So on November 15, families would bring all three-year-old children, five-year-old girls, and seven-year-old boys to the local shrine for blessings of good health and continued growth. Many Japanese still continue this tradition today.

At all festivals, including the ones mentioned above, people enjoy celebrating special events and sharing traditions of the past with new generations. People carry portable shrines in parades. They dance and play drums, flutes, and bells. Many Japanese like to wear traditional kimonos on these special days as well.

Questions and Activities

1. How are the traditions for New Year's in Japan similar to those in China? How do you celebrate New Year's?

2. If you could make a special holiday just for girls or just for boys, what would that holiday be? Give your holiday a name and date and organize special activities for the occasion. Share ideas as a class and vote on one "Girl's Day" and one "Boy's Day."

3. Draw a large carp on a sheet of white construction paper and cut it out. Glue on pieces of colored tissue paper, using liquid starch and a paintbrush. Do the same on the backside. Once dry, outline the carp with black permanent marker and add on details. If desired, fasten on colored tissue paper streamers to the tail. Tie a string at the mouth end and then hang your carp on a pole outside your classroom to swim in the breeze.

A Land of Volcanic Unrest

Millions of years ago, volcanic eruptions shoved gigantic mountains up out of the ocean. The tops of these mountains became the islands of Japan. Mountains run down the middle of every island in Japan, covering approximately three-quarters of the land. The largest island, Honshu, contains most of Japan's highest mountains, including the famous Mount Fuji.

Like most of Japan's mountains, Mount Fuji is a volcano. Although it has not erupted since 1707, about 70 of Japan's other volcanoes are currently active and pose a threat to the country. The world's largest volcano, Mount Aso, is on the southern island of Kyushu.

Scientists in Japan study many aspects of their volcanoes, including lava viscosity. Viscosity is a liquid's internal friction or ability to flow fast or slow. Water is a liquid with low viscosity, and so it flows freely. Liquids such as honey and maple syrup both have high viscosity, making them thick and slow moving. By studying the viscosity of lava, scientists can determine how dangerous an active volcano might be. It is the amount of silica in the lava that determines its viscosity. A volcano with small amounts of silica has a low viscosity. It is swift moving and able to destroy surrounding areas quickly without much time for evacuation. The more silica in the lava, the thicker and slower it flows.

By studying the lava viscosity, scientists can also determine the type of volcano that will be formed. For example, the lava from Mount St. Helens is highly viscous, and so the slow-moving lava created a steep-sided volcano. On the other hand, the lava found in the Hawaiian Islands is thin and swift moving, creating flat volcanoes.

Try This Experiment

1. Gather four clear household liquids with a variety of viscosity (cooking oil, vinegar, shampoo, liquid soap, corn syrup, molasses, honey, baby oil, etc.).

2. Pour the same amount of each liquid into four tall, clear beakers or graduated cylinders. Label the beakers A, B, C, and D. Imagine the four samples are lava taken from four different volcanoes in Japan. It is your job as the scientist to test the lava viscosity and report to the public the dangers posed by each volcano.

3. Use a stopwatch and four marbles to test the lava's viscosity and record your findings on the charts on page 54. Begin with sample A. Describe the liquid and then time how long it takes for a marble to drop through the liquid to the bottom of the container. Record your finding on the chart. Based on the speed of the marble, predict the amount of silica in this lava sample and record your prediction on the chart by placing an "X" along the scale and drawing a picture of the volcano that would be formed.

4. Continue this procedure with the three other lava samples. Then make a report to the people living in the areas around each of the volcanoes. What kind of warning would each receive?

   Sample A_____

   Sample B_____

   Sample C_____

   Sample D_____

A Land of Volcanic Unrest *(cont.)*

Viscosity Data Sheet

Sample A

Describe the lava sample.

_____

Viscosity rating in_____seconds

Circle the amount of silica in this lava.

More Silica   Less Silica

├┼┼┼┼┼┼┼┼┼┼┼┼┼┤

Draw an illustration of the kind of volcano that might have this type of lava.

Sample B

Describe the lava sample.

_____

Viscosity rating in_____seconds

Circle the amount of silica in this lava.

More Silica   Less Silica

├┼┼┼┼┼┼┼┼┼┼┼┼┼┤

Draw an illustration of the kind of volcano that might have this type of lava.

Sample C

Describe the lava sample.

_____

Viscosity rating in_____seconds

Circle the amount of silica in this lava.

More Silica   Less Silica

├┼┼┼┼┼┼┼┼┼┼┼┼┼┤

Draw an illustration of the kind of volcano that might have this type of lava.

Sample D

Describe the lava sample.

_____

Viscosity rating in_____seconds

Circle the amount of silica in this lava.

More Silica   Less Silica

├┼┼┼┼┼┼┼┼┼┼┼┼┼┤

Draw an illustration of the kind of volcano that might have this type of lava.

Ring of Fire

About 8,000 earthquakes strike Japan every year. Most of these tremors are so small that they are ignored, but occasionally the quakes are big enough to cause damage. One of the biggest earthquakes in recent years hit Kobe, a port city on Honshu, in 1995. Over 5,000 people were killed, over 26,000 people were injured, and more than 56,000 structures were damaged or completely destroyed. Many times the earthquake is accompanied by a huge tidal wave called a tsunami, which also causes great damage. It is Japan's location that makes it prone to earthquakes and volcanic eruptions, for Japan sits near a plate boundary of the ring of fire. Complete the following map activity to view these plate boundaries and their relation to Japan.

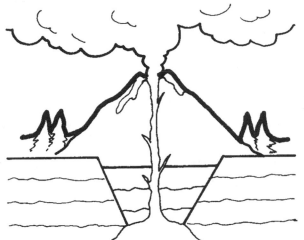

Preparing for the Lesson:

1. Reproduce the Ring of Fire Map (page 57) and Locating the Ring of Fire (page 56) for students.

2. Make an overhead transparency of the Ring of Fire Map (page 57) to show students how to locate points on the map using latitude and longitude.

Teaching the Lesson:

1. Discuss the definitions of an earthquake and a volcano with students.

2. Ask students to share experiences they have had with earthquakes or volcanic eruptions.

3. Distribute the Ring of Fire Map (page 57) and Locating the Ring of Fire (page 56). Review the difference between latitude and longitude.

4. Using the overhead transparency of the Ring of Fire Map (page 57), model for students how to locate some of the points on the map.

5. Assign the maps as homework or allow time for students to complete them in class.

6. Discuss students' findings. You may wish to ask the following questions to help guide the discussion: Why do you think the term *ring of fire* is used? Where would you expect future earthquakes and volcanoes to occur? Where do you think the safest places would be to avoid the possibility of earthquakes and volcanoes? What can people do to protect themselves from earthquakes and/or volcanoes?

7. You may wish to have students bring in other sources of information related to earthquakes and volcanic activity. *Earthquake* by Seymour Simon (Morrow, 1991) is an excellent resource.

8. If you live close to an Imax or Omnimax Theater, you might consider going on a field trip to see the movie *Ring of Fire*.

9. Extend this activity by having students write a story about being in an earthquake or near a volcanic eruption.

Ring of Fire *(cont.)*

Locating the Ring of Fire

Use a blue crayon to mark the following earthquake locations on the map (page 57).

Earthquake	Latitude	Longitude
1	55º S	55º W
2	50º S	75º W
3	25º S	75º W
4	10º S	105º E
5	5º S	150º E
6	0º	80º W
7	15º N	105º W
8	15º N	100º E
9	20º N	75º W
10	20º N	60º E
11	30º N	60º E
12	30º N	115º W
13	35º N	35º E
14	40º N	20º E
15	40º N	0º
16	40º N	145º E
17	45º N	125º W
18	50º N	158º E
19	60º N	135º W
20	60º N	152º W

Use a red crayon to mark the following volcano locations.

Volcano	Latitude	Longitude
1	5º S	105º E
2	5º S	155º E
3	10º S	120º E
4	15º S	60º E
5	0º	75º W
6	17º N	25º W
7	20º N	155º W
8	20º N	105º W
9	30º N	60º E
10	40º N	30º W
11	40º N	30º E
12	40º N	145º E
13	45º N	15º E
14	45º N	120º W
15	55º N	160º E
16	60º N	150º W
17	65º N	15º E

Ring of Fire *(cont.)*

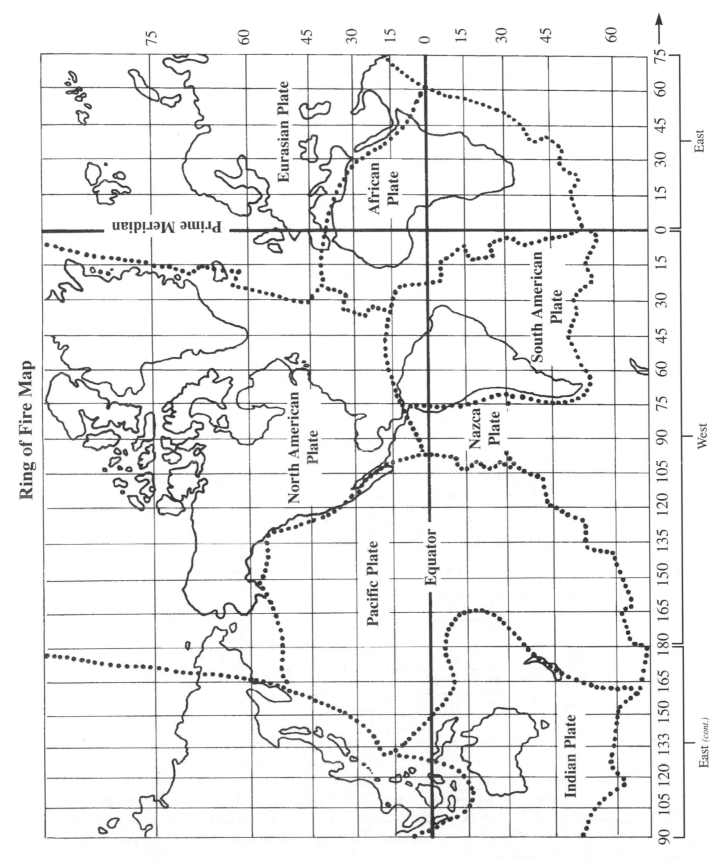

Ring of Fire Map

Japanese Strategy Games

The Japanese love playing games of logic and strategy with words, military figurines, and/or numbers. The three number games below let you test your skill in logic and strategy. They can be introduced by the teacher playing against the entire class on the chalkboard or overhead projector. Once students understand how to play, they can play in pairs.

Guess My Number: Choose a three-digit number with no repeating digits. For example, 308 is okay but 338 is not. Have a friend try to guess your number as you give clues. A sample game is played below.

(The number they are trying to guess is *421*. It took 6 guesses to figure out the number.)

Guess		You Write:
1.	513	1 number correct, 0 digits in the right place
2.	756	0 numbers correct
3.	324	2 numbers correct, 1 digit in the right place
4.	348	1 number correct, 0 digits in the right place
5.	124	3 numbers correct, 1 digit in the right place
6.	421	3 numbers correct, 3 digits in the right place

Take turns at selecting and guessing numbers. The player who guesses the number in the least amount of turns is the winner. As an extension, try a four-digit number.

Target 50: This game is played with two dice. The object of the game is to come as close as possible to 50 without ever going over. Each player will get 10 rolls of the dice. Before each roll they will need to decide whether they are going to add the number on the dice to their total or subtract it. A sample game is played below:

Player 1

Roll	Decision	Outcome	Total
1	add	10	0+10=10
2	add	5	10+5=15
3	add	11	15+11=26
4	add	9	26+9=35
5	add	8	35+8=43
6	subtract	6	43-6=37
7	add	7	37+7=44
8	subtract	11	44-11=33
9	add	4	33+4=37
10	add	9	37+9=46

Player 2

Roll	Decision	Outcome	Total
1	add	4	0+4=4
2	add	6	4+6=10
3	add	6	10+6=16
4	add	9	16+9=25
5	add	4	25+4=29
6	add	6	29+6=35
7	add	5	35+5=40
8	subtract	6	40-6=34
9	add	7	34+7=41
10	subtract	12	41-12=29

Player 1 is the winner. Have students play several times to gain a sense of strategy.

Target 100: This game is played the same as the game above with ten rolls of the dice being added or subtracted. However, this time you will multiply the two dice instead of adding them together. For example, if you roll a 5 and a 2, it becomes 5 x 2, or 10. If you roll a 6 and a 4, it becomes 6 x 4, or 24. The object of the game is to come as close to 100 as possible without ever going over.

The Hour of the Dog

In ancient Japan, time was told not with numbers but with animals. On the clock below, traditional Japanese animal symbols replace the usual numbers. Refer to this clock to answer the following questions.

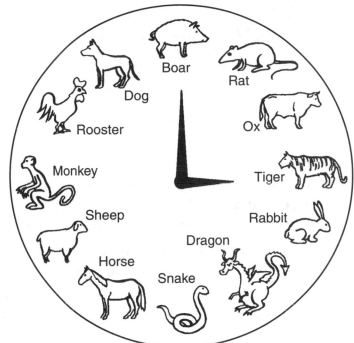

1. At what hour do you wake up?

   _____

2. At what hour do you start school?

   _____

3. At what hour do you eat lunch?

   _____

4. If you eat dinner around the hour of the snake, how many hours pass until you go to bed?

   _____

5. If it is now the hour of the ox and you must be home by the hour of the dragon, how long do you have left to be with your friends?

   _____

Activity: Make a daily school schedule based on the animal clock above. Write down the names of your subjects and teachers at the time they occur. Try to use this ancient time system all day when talking to friends or teachers about your schedule and plans.

The Hour of the Horse

_____

The Hour of the Sheep

_____

The Hour of the Monkey

_____

The Hour of the Rooster

_____

The Hour of the Dog

_____

The Hour of the Boar

_____

The Hour of the Rat

_____

The Hour of the Ox

_____

The Hour of the Tiger

_____

The Hour of the Rabbit

_____

Why is this time system not as efficient as our own? Give at least three reasons.

1. _____

2. _____

3. _____

Jomon Pots

The early Jomon culture takes its name from its distinctive pottery created by pressing cords into wet clay. Have your students create Jomon artifacts to display in your classroom.

Materials:

- strands of heavy string, twine, rope, or cord
- white or red clay (Each student should get a ball the size of a baseball.)
- paper or plastic to cover the work area
- pictures of Jomon pottery

Directions:

1. Display the pictures of Jomon pottery found in resource books. Have students note the primitive shapes and simplistic features. Discuss the relief patterns made on the pots by pressing cords into the wet clay. The cord patterns are plain and knotted to give a variation.

2. Cover the work areas and distribute the clay and strands to students. Have students form their balls of clay into simple pot shapes by pressing their thumbs in the middle and pinching out the sides.

3. Have students create a cord pattern on their pots. It may be all uniform or alternating and with or without knots. Let students experiment with pressing the cords into the wet clay.

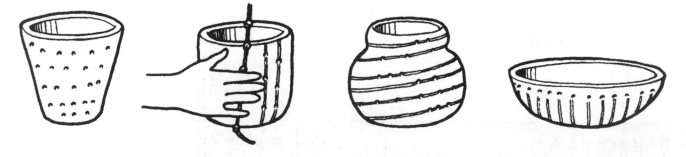

4. Once their pots are completed, have students carve their names into the bottoms of their pots using a pencil. Set the pot out to dry. If desired, after a few days fire the pots in a kiln, following the kiln directions.

5. Make a Jomon pot display to compare the different techniques, shapes, and styles of your pots.

Bunraku Puppets

Bunraku is the ancient art of Japanese puppet theater. The puppets are four feet tall and designed with precise details in facial expression and costuming. Unlike marionettes that dangle on strings in front of a curtain, the bunraku puppets and their puppeteers walk around on a stage. The puppeteers are dressed in black from head to toe to blend in with the background. One person, who uses a different tone of voice for each puppet, tells the story. Music is provided by the samisen, a traditional three-stringed instrument.

Conduct your own bunraku puppet shows by following the directions below. The stories can be written by the students or taken from Japanese literature and fairy tales.

Directions for Creating a Bunraku Puppet Show:

1. Divide the class into groups of four. Each group will select or compose a story and create puppets to tell their story. Each story should be from 5–10 minutes long.

2. Have students write out their story like a script. One student will be telling the story and reading the parts for all of the puppets. The other three students will be working the puppets on top of a table as if it were stage.

3. Allow time for students to practice with their scripts and puppets. If desired, students may accompany their presentation with music, using a portable tape player.

4. Once students are prepared, set up the final stage in the front of the classroom by covering the front wall and table or stage with black butcher paper. Have the puppeteers dress all in black for their performance. If possible, turn off the classroom lights and use an overhead projector as a spotlight during the performances.

Directions for Making the Bunraku Puppets:

1. Reproduce pages 62 and 63 for each student. Have each student plan the costume for his or her puppet based on the story selected for the puppet show. Use the samples on page 63 as well as pictures from resource books. Make a sample to show students the finished product.

2. Cut out the puppet pattern on page 62 and glue it onto poster board. Then cut out the pattern again and attach the arm at the elbow and shoulder with brads.

3. Tape a bamboo skewer to the back of the puppet. Tape the hand to a bamboo skewer to create a moveable arm.

4. Have students use construction paper and/or patterned wrapping paper to design the hair, hats, clothing, and shoes. Draw on facial features and other details, using markers. Make sure both the front and the back of the puppet is clothed and decorated.

5. Remind students to cut around the brads when gluing on the puppet costumes. Have students check to make sure the one arm is left mobile for gesturing during the show.

Bunraku Puppets *(cont.)*

Use the outline below to create your Bunraku puppet. You will need poster board, scissors, glue, two brads, and two bamboo skewers, markers, and construction paper.

1. Cut out the outline.

2. Glue it to poster board and cut out the pieces again.

3. Attach the upper and lower arm using brads. Tape the skewers to the hand and the back.

4. Create hair and a costume for the puppet using construction paper and/or patterned wrapping paper.

5. Add facial features and details with markers.

6. Make sure you have decorated the front and back of the puppet and that the arm moves freely.

Bunraku Puppets *(cont.)*

Use the examples below to design your puppet. Choose a hairstyle, facial expression, and costume that will enhance your story.

Peasant Farmer   Peasant Woman   Noble Woman   Noble Woman

Warrior monk   Buddhist   Nobleman   Samurai

Create a Medieval Castle

Japanese feudal lords built fortified castles during the 16th and 17th centuries. The design of these fortress-palaces included barred windows, gates, trapdoors, and vantage points for firing guns and arrows. One fine example of this period architecture is the Himeji Castle. Also known as the White Heron Castle, it was built in 1557 during the civil wars that preceded the Tokugawa period. Have students create their own Japanese castles to better understand the art of Japanese architecture. Make a castle display on a bulletin board.

Materials:

- white construction paper, black fine-line permanent ink marker, pencil, scissors, black construction paper, glue, watercolor paints, water, and a paintbrush

- examples from resource books of Japanese architecture showing the pagoda-style castles

Directions:

1. Have students examine a variety of Japanese architectural styles in resource books. Discuss the interesting shapes of the roof layers. Then distribute the drawing materials.

2. Divide the paper into four to five sections horizontally to create the layers of the castle.

3. Use a pencil to draw in the roof outline at the different layers. Add windows, doors, a rock foundation, gable decorations, etc.

4. Use a fine-line marker to outline all of the details.

5. Use the watercolors to paint different sections of the castle. Students should choose two or three different colors for the color scheme of the painting. The majority of the castle should be left white.

6. Once dry, cut out the castle and glue it to a sheet of black construction paper. Write the name of the castle and the student's name on the front. Use a white pencil or marker, or provide blank adhesive address labels.

7. Display the castles on a bulletin board or use them as a border around the room.

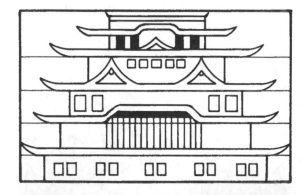

A Classroom Meditation Garden

The art of landscape gardening came to Japan from China. The beauty of gardens and courtyards was as important as the architecture of the buildings themselves. With the rising influence of Zen Buddhism during the Ashikaga period, the design and maintenance of gardens reached new heights. Temple gardens were designed to foster meditation and create a feeling of calm and tranquility. Everything contained in the garden had some symbolic meaning. Ornamental trees such as pines, camellias, flowering plums, and bamboo were placed strategically within a field of white raked sand, gnarled volcanic rocks, moss, ponds, and lakes. Pathways and bridges led the way to wooded groves or tea-ceremony pavilions.

Have your class create and maintain a Zen meditation garden, following the directions below. Allow one group of students to build the original garden, and then rotate groups to rearrange and rake the garden sands every week.

Materials

- 1 large box top (apple box top, ditto paper box top, etc.)
- sand to fill the box top at least 1 inch (2.54 cm) deep
- 2–3 baseball sized rocks
- any other garden ornaments desired (miniature shrub, sculpture, etc.)
- 1 wide-tooth comb to "rake" the garden sands

Directions:

1. Ask students if they have ever seen a Japanese garden before. Many cities have local botanical gardens, museums, or restaurants that contain a Japanese style garden with raked sand. Show pictures of Japanese gardens from resource books. Have the students note that the gardens are not lush and filled with many plants, but simple and serene.

2. Tell students that they will all get a turn to be the classroom temple gardeners. Divide the class into gardening groups with about four students in each group.

3. Give the supplies to the first group and allow them to pour in the sand, place the rocks, and rake the sand to their desired design.

4. Place the garden in a section of the room for all to enjoy. Each week assign a different group to rearrange and rake the garden. What makes this type of garden enjoyable? Is it peaceful to look at? Is it enjoyable to maintain?

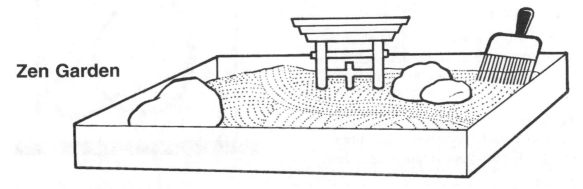

Zen Garden

Zen Painting

As with many other art forms, Japanese painting was originally influenced by the Chinese and later developed its own characteristics. Paintings were usually created on paper or silks, using ink and/or watercolors. Most paintings were displayed as scrolls, screens, panels, and fans. Subjects for paintings included nature scenes with plants or animals, highly detailed narrative scenes depicting urban life, battles, court life, literature themes, and portraits. Another style of painting emerged during the rise of Zen Buddhism, which emphasized the beauty of simplicity. This style created images with only a few rapid brush strokes, using only black ink.

Create your own Zen work of art, following the directions below:

1. Choose a subject to practice the Zen style of art—a tree, flower, cat, house, horse, etc.

2. Instead of a detailed drawing of the subject, try to depict the image with only a few pencil strokes. For example, look at the two images of a cat below.

3. Once you have chosen a subject and have practiced the strokes with your pencil on some scratch paper, you are ready to paint your picture.

4. Gather a sheet of white copy paper, black tempera paint (thinned with water), and a large watercolor paintbrush.

5. Using the few strokes you have practiced, paint your subject on the paper. Using a thin red marker, write your name in the corner as shown in the example.

6. Once the paper is dry, glue a strip of black paper to the top and bottom to make it look like a scroll. Hang your painting with a piece of yarn.

7. Examine the other Zen paintings and see if the images are clearly portrayed with only a few strokes. Discuss your findings as a class.

Print a Family Mon

In Japanese society the nobles and their families held the highest rank. Each family had its own distinctive *mon*, or badge, to designate its heritage. Mons were used on articles of clothing and military gear and as seals. To transfer the mon onto paper, a block printing technique was used.

First, an artist prepared an original drawing with black ink on translucent paper. A craftsman pasted it facedown to a smooth block of wood. With a sharp knife, he cut through the paper into the wood, following each line carefully. The background was then chipped away with a chisel and mallet. Next, a printer rolled his black printing ink onto the raised surface of the wood, placed a piece of paper on top, and rubbed the back of the paper with a pad. When he peeled off the paper, the design was transferred onto it. A great number of prints could be made from the same block in this way.

Follow the directions below to print your own family mon, using a similar printing technique.

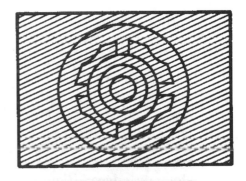

Materials: 2 sheets of 9" x 12" (23 x 30 cm) black construction paper, 1 sheet of red 9" x 12" (23 x 30 cm) construction paper, 3 large index cards, pencil, scissors, glue, white acrylic paint, and a paintbrush

1. On one sheet of the black paper, draw your family crest or mon.

2. Using the index cards, cut pieces to cover selected areas of your design. You can add more than one layer, but remember to cut along each edge of the design in order for it to print.

3. Glue the index card pieces to the design on the sheet of black construction paper. Cut out the design and let it fully dry.

4. Once it is dry, paint a thin layer of the white acrylic paint onto the design. Make sure the work surface is covered with paper or plastic so that you can paint out to the very edge. (**Note:** Acrylic paint will stain clothes. Wear protective clothing and wash paint out immediately.)

5. Working quickly so that the paint does not dry, turn the design onto the clean sheet of black construction paper and evenly rub the back to transfer the design. Peel the top sheet off carefully.

6. Allow the paint to dry, and then cut around the edge of the mon, leaving a $\frac{1}{4}$" (.6 cm) black border. Glue the finished product to the red construction paper. Trim the edge to form a red border around the entire mon and display it.

Make a Screen or Fan

Some of the most treasured subjects of Japanese art are objects of nature. These subjects adorn paper screens and fans used throughout the Orient. Look through books of Japanese art to get some ideas on plants, trees, bamboo, animals, seasons, and water. Then choose one of the lessons below to depict your nature scene.

A Japanese Screen

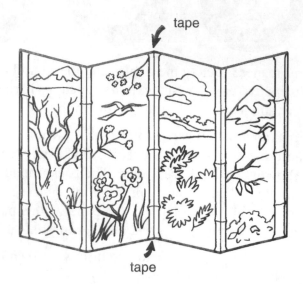

Materials: 2 sheets of 12" x 9" (30 x 23 cm) white construction paper, tape, colored markers

1. Tape the two sheets of construction paper together vertically. Fold the paper to form four sections.

2. Draw a bamboo frame around each section.

3. On each panel draw a nature picture depicting one of the four seasons. Color the pictures and display them.

A Japanese Fan

Materials: 5 sheets of white copy paper, tape, and colored markers

1. Lay the five sheets of paper next to each other and design your nature scene so that it flows from one page onto the other. You may want the design to begin on the middle sheet and radiate toward the edges. Color the design with markers. Use color to add a wide border around the perimeter of the five sheets of paper.

2. Fold each of the sheets back and forth like a fan. Staple the sheets together at the base and tape along the edges. If desired, tie a ribbon or tassel at the base. Spread out the fan to display on a bulletin board.

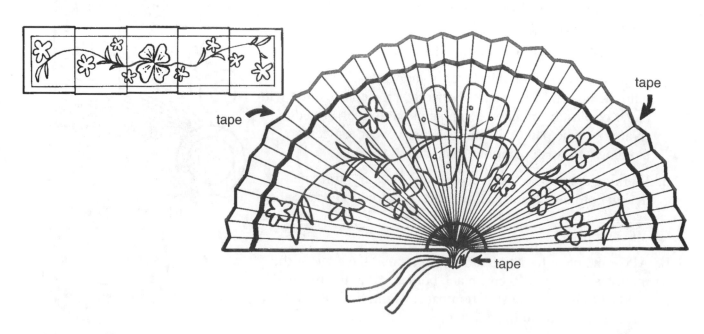

Plan a Noh Play

Kabuki and *Noh* are Japan's oldest forms of drama. In Kabuki theater, the actors wear elaborate costumes and heavy makeup. They perform against a backdrop of lavish, colorful scenery. These dramas last about five hours and are filled with sword fights, dances, and music. Sometimes at the end of the play the hero will stare and cross his eyes, which is considered a special kind of beauty. Like the traditional Greek dramas, male actors play both the male and female roles.

Noh theater is also performed by an all-male cast. However, in this art form the actors wear highly expressive masks and elaborate traditional costumes. The drama is performed on a simple stage with no scenery or props. The story is told with special dramatic movements of slow dance steps to the music of drums and flutes and the chanting of poetry. There are five subjects for Noh plays: the gods, historical battles, beautiful women, devils, and present-day events. In ancient times, Noh plays were performed for the wealthy elite while Kabuki was for the common people.

Directions for planning a Noh Play:

1. Divide the class into groups of 4–6 students. Have each group choose a popular slow song for their drama that is school-appropriate and approved by the teacher. Based on the lyrics of their song, have students choose one of the five types of Noh plays to depict.

2. Have students write out a summary of their play to be read before the performance. There will be no speaking during the play, so students will need to practice exaggerating their gestures and movements to the audience to convey what is happening. Remind students to make their movements slow and to choreograph them to the music.

3. Have students use white paper plates and black markers to make expressive masks appropriate for their performances. Make sure the students can see out of the eyeholes once the mask is tied into place.

4. Allow time for the groups to practice their plays together. On the day of the performance, clear an empty stage at the front of the room. After each performance, discuss how well the group conveyed the plot of their play through movement and music only. Were their masks helpful? Discuss this type of performance and how it compares to other types of drama such as opera, musical theater, dance performances, ballet, etc.

Conduct a Tea Ceremony

The tea plant came to Japan from China during the Heian period. Ordinary tea was served at most family meals. Zen Buddhist monasteries began serving a special powdered green tea in beautiful drinking bowls, following an elaborate set of rituals. A small number of friends would meet for this tea-drinking ceremony, during which they admired a work of art, recited poetry, or discussed ideas. The ceremony could last from one to four hours. This type of gathering became so popular in the Ashikaga period that special tearooms were built into houses and gardens solely for the purpose of the tea-drinking ceremony. Today, people around the world study the of tea ceremony, learning the intricate rituals for host and guest, seeking truth and peace. There are several different schools that teach the tea ceremony, and there are different types of ceremonies. In some, a meal is served, while in others a sweet accompanies the tea. Each person involved follows a strict set of rules for proper behavior.

The traditional tearoom is simple. There is a hearth for the tea preparation and an alcove for displaying a flower arrangement or work of art. The door is built low to the ground so that those entering must lower their heads, a sign of humility. The floor is covered with *tatami* or rush mats, which also serve as seating. A stone lantern and a water basin are usually placed near the entrance.

The utensils for the tea ceremony are chosen with great care. A decorated iron kettle with two handles and no spout is used to heat the water. The pottery chosen for the tea jar and bowl follows the principles of Zen Buddhism, with simple, eye-pleasing shapes. Many households use lacquer-ware for the ceremony.

The tea or, *o-cha,* used in the ceremony is a variety called *matcha.* Although it comes from the same plant as other more familiar teas, it is made from younger, fresher leaves. Most teas are allowed to dry and ferment, which gives them their characteristic color and flavor. Green tea is less processed than other teas. In a tea ceremony, the tea may be prepared as *koi-cha,* a thick, strong beverage. In this ceremony all guests drink from a single bowl. *Usu-cha,* or weak tea, may also be prepared. This is served in individual bowls.

Conduct a Tea Ceremony *(cont.)*

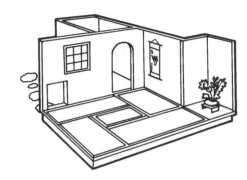

The ceremony is conducted by a host (owner of the tearoom) and a tea master. The tea master may be the host or the host's wife or daughter. Before entering the tearoom, guests scoop water out of the basin with a bamboo dipper and wash their hands and mouths. This purifies them for the ceremony. Wooden clappers are sounded as the signal to enter the tea pavilion. Guests crawl into the room on hands and knees. They bow to their host and sit on the mats in a circle.

Once everyone is seated, the tea master heats the water in the kettle. He or she then takes a small amount of green powder from the tea jar and places it into the drinking bowl. Hot water is scooped out of the kettle with a dipper and poured over the tea powder. The mixture is beaten to a froth with a bamboo whisk called a *chasen*. The tea bowl is placed in front of the guests.

(**Note:** To decaffeinate tea, pour boiling water over tea leaves and steep for 10–15 seconds. Pour off the water and discard it. Use the tea leaves again; they will now be decaffeinated. Commercial decaffeinated tea or another beverage may also be used.)

Tea Drinking Etiquette and Instructions

Place the tea bowl outside the border of the tatami on which you are sitting.

If there is a guest who has been served before you, it is polite to bow and say "Please let me accompany you."

Next, bow and excuse yourself for going first to any guest who has not yet been served.

Turn to the host, bow, and address him with the words, "I will partake of your tea."

Pick up the bowl with your right hand and place it on the palm of your left hand. Put the fingers of your right hand around it, with the thumb facing you, and make a small bow for politeness.

With the bowl still resting on the palm of your left hand, grasp the rim of the bowl with your forefinger and thumb and turn it about ninety degrees clockwise. Take a sip and then comment on how good it tastes, while dropping your right hand on the tatami before your knees.

Drink the remaining tea in small sips and when you come to the last sip, inhale deeply, make an audible sound and finish the tea.

After you drink, the rim of the bowl should be wiped lightly with tissue paper from left to right as you hold the bowl between your forefinger and thumb. With the bowl still resting on your left palm, turn it counterclockwise so that it returns to the same position it was in before you drank from it. This is done with the thumb at the edge of the bowl and the other four fingers underneath it.

Place the bowl on the outside of the tatami border and with your hands on the mat gaze at the bowl to appreciate its shape. The bowl can be picked up with both hands to view it more closely.

Pick up the bowl and return it to the host. The bowl should be turned twice, in a quarter circle (90°) each time, so that the front of the bowl faces the host when you return it to him or her.

It is considered polite to admire the tea implements and to ask the host about his selection of tea.

During the ceremony conversation revolves around art, poetry, and enlightened ideas. No trivial gossip or flattery is permitted. Sometimes music is played for the guests, or there may even be a dance performance. At the end of the ceremony, bow to the host and back out of the room, being careful not to step on the tatami mat.

Famous People and Places

Make a poster describing the background and contributions of one of the following people or places. Use the example below as your guide.

Famous People in Japanese History

- Toyotomi Hideyosh
- Jimmu Tenno
- Empress Suiko Tenno
- Prince Shotoku Taishi
- Fujiware-Naskatomi Kamatari
- Sesshu
- Tokugawa Ieyasu
- Izanagi and Izanami
- Yoritomo Minamoto
- Oda Nobunaga
- Lady Murasaki Shikibu

Famous Places in Japanese History

- Nara
- Heian-kyo (Kyoto)
- Edo (Tokyo)
- Kamakura
- Mount Fuji
- Osaka
- Nagasaki
- Kobe

Once your poster is complete, give a brief oral presentation about your famous person or place. Use your poster and other props as visual aids.

The Samurai

Background Information:

Code of Conduct:

Duties:

Contributions to Japanese Culture:

by Kara James

A Day in Ancient Japan

With the class, recreate a day in the life of the ancient Japanese. Begin to plan for this day at least two weeks in advance. You may wish to team with another class or an entire grade level to share in this special day. Parents may also enjoy participating in all or some of the activities. After you have decided on a schedule of events, you may wish to write a letter to parents, inviting them to participate.

Suggested Activities:

1. Encourage students to dress as ancient Japanese for the day. At least one week before the event, display pictures of typical Japanese attire (pages 75–76). Discuss the ideas presented on pages 75–76 and give each student a copy to take home.

2. Ask students to bring in items to create a Japanese feast. Review page 74 for ideas. Many of these foods can be purchased in the International section of the grocery store. Because Japanese food may be quite different from your students' usual diet, review the food choices and alter as needed. For example, canned tuna can be used as raw fish, heated chicken broth can replace miso soup, and carrot and celery sticks can be used for the pickled vegetables. Bring in sets of chopsticks and encourage students to eat their meals following the etiquette guidelines. Schedule the feast near or in place of the lunch period. Have students sit on the floor or at their desks and play traditional Japanese music during the feast. (Check your library or music store for music.)

3. As an alternative, check with local Japanese restaurants about providing a low-cost meal in exchange for good advertising. If you have Japanese students in your class, ask them and their families to participate in the feast by sharing their favorite traditional recipes.

4. Adorn the classroom with Torii Gates (page 78) and Japanese art made by the students.

5. Have groups of students perform their Bunraku puppet shows (pages 61–63) or Noh plays (page 69).

6. Create a work of Japanese art (pages 66–68).

7. Play a Japanese strategy game (page 58).

8. Write Japanese poetry (page 39), practice writing Japanese (page 42), and share Japanese fairy tales (pages 36–38).

A Day in Ancient Japan *(cont.)*

Japanese Food

Rice is considered the most important food item in Japan. The rice used in Japanese cooking is a short-grained, semi-transparent variety that becomes slightly sticky when cooked. Even the names of the daily meals contain the word rice. Most people eat rice with every meal along with hot green tea. Below are some traditional foods that also accompany meals in Japan:

Asa-Gohan (morning rice, or breakfast)

miso (mee-so) soup—a broth with tofu, made from soybean paste

pickled vegetables

eggs

Hiru-gohan (noon rice, or lunch) or Ban-gohan or (night rice, or dinner)

udon (ooh-dahn)—thick wheat noodles in broth

soba (so-ba)—thick buckwheat noodles in broth

sushi (soo-shee)—bite-sized cakes of vinegar rice with raw fish/seaweed/vegetables/eggs dipped in soy sauce

sashimi (sa-shee-mee)—raw fish seaweed

tempura (tem-poo-rah)—battered and fried seafood and vegetables dipped in a tempura sauce

tofu (toe-foo)—bean curd

pickled vegetables

oranges and melon

The way food looks is as important as its freshness and taste in Japan. Food is served in an artistic display on small dishes on a tray. The Japanese eat with chopsticks rather than silverware, following a strict set of etiquette rules:

1. Before eating, bow your head and say *Itadakimasu* (Ee-tah-dah-kee-mahs-u), which means "I receive" or a blessing of thanks for the food.

2. When taking food from the same serving dish as others, turn the chopsticks around and use the ends that have not been in your mouth.

3. There are strict rules for the use of chopsticks.

   Do not grab chopsticks with your fist, or wave them in the air or over food.

   Do not stick them in a piece of food or use them to pass food from person to person or use them to dig through a shared dish to find the best piece.

   Never stick them upright in your rice. (This is the way rice is offered to the dead at the family shrine.)

4. To eat soup or rice, pick up the bowl so that it is close to your mouth. Pick the solids out of soup with the chopsticks and then drink the soup out of the bowl like a cup. Make sure you slurp your soup—it's a sign of a good appetite.

5. At the end of the meal, place your chopsticks neatly on the chopstick rest or across the dish closest to you.

A Day in Ancient Japan *(cont.)*

Japanese Clothing

As in any culture, the style of Japanese dress has gone through a number of changes over time. Choose examples from pictures in books and any of the time periods below to design your costume. Use regular household items such as robes, scarves, pants, pajamas, sandals, and thongs. Be creative with hairstyles, cosmetics, and additional accessories.

The typical Japanese kimono was a relatively late development. During the third to eighth centuries, both men and women wore a two-piece costume with a jacket that flared out over the hips. Men wore wide trousers while women wore pleated skirts. Working-class people wore clothing made from hemp, linen, or cotton, while silk was preferred by the wealthy.

From the Nara to Heian periods, clothing of the upper class was influenced by Chinese culture. For outdoor activities, men wore black trousers and silk tunics, covered by a flowing silk robe in bright colors. Indoors they wore robes closed with a wide sash. Women's clothing became extremely elaborate during this time. Upper class women wore loose silk trousers. Over the top they wore several silk robes of different colors, arranged so that the layers were visible at the hem, sleeves, and neckline. The number of robes and colors allowed depended on one's status.

During the Kamakura period, around the twelfth century, clothing became simplified. This was due to the rise of the samurai military class and the decline of the old aristocracy. Although the women wore fewer layers, they were still colorful and costly. Outside the home, women were expected to cover themselves with large, plain outer robes and wear large hats with veils that covered their faces. Men wore wide flat trousers, a robe as an undergarment, and a stiff jacket that flared at the shoulders and hips.

A Day in Ancient Japan *(cont.)*

Japanese Clothing *(cont.)*

The kimono became popular during the Ashikaga period, around the fourteenth to fifteenth centuries. This was a long, flowing robe worn with a broad sash. Men's and women's kimonos were distinguished by subtle differences in cut and color. Although the garments were simple in style, they required elaborate weaving and dying techniques.

During the Tokugawa period, from the seventeenth to nineteenth centuries, the shogunal government tried to restrict expensive and colorful kimonos to only the samurai class. The common people obeyed and wore plain outer garments, although wealthy town dwellers lined the insides of their garments with colorful and expensive silks.

In rural areas, the style of dress did not change much over time. Both men and women peasants wore trousers and jackets. Women also wore aprons and headscarfs. The most common color was indigo blue, and sometimes a block printing technique was used to produce patterns of blue and white.

Outdoors, all Japanese wore sandals woven from rice straw. To avoid mud in wet regions, a raised wooden clog or thong called a *geta* was worn.

Both men and women in the upper class wore cosmetics at different periods of time. Powder was used to whiten the face, rouge colored the cheeks and lips, and a vegetable dye was used to paint nails. Women shaved their eyebrows and used black powder to paint in artificial "moth wing" eyebrows. Clothing was scented with perfume from incense, and women grew their hair exceptionally long to be done up into fancy hairstyles with carved and gilded combs. Fans and parasols were carried by both men and women.

Organizational Folders/Journals

Three different books have been presented for this thematic unit on ancient Japan. Make individual folders for each book, or combine all of the units together into one organizational folder so that students can record information, take notes, and organize their materials.

1. Fold a sheet of construction paper in half for the cover. Have each student decorate the cover with the title of the book, author, and his or her name. Draw an appropriate picture for the cover.

2. Reproduce appropriate student pages for the unit (vocabulary lists, maps, comprehension questions, etc.) for each journal.

3. Assemble the journals by punching holes into the construction paper covers and using brads. This will allow students to add other pages they complete as the unit progresses. Place the reproduced sheets and at least ten pages of blank writing paper into each journal and secure with the brads.

4. As you complete each reading selection, have students define words from their vocabulary lists that appeared in their reading. On a separate page, have them write a brief summary of what happened in the section and their thoughts and feelings. Have students write predictions in their journals of what they think will happen in the next chapters. Check to see if predictions came true.

5. Make sure students are labeling each section in their journals by the chapters covered. As other activities from this unit are completed, punch holes in the pages and add them to the appropriate sections of the journals.

Ancient Japan Bulletin Board

Make a map of Japan on a large circle of red butcher paper, using an opaque projector and the image on page 46. Cover the bulletin board with white butcher paper and place the red circle containing the map in the center so that the bulletin board resembles the Japanese flag. Cut a large half-circle out of yellow butcher paper and zigzag the edge so that it resembles a fan. Label as shown and place onto the bulletin board. Use black Oriental-style letters to title the bulletin board. As the unit progresses, add information to the fan-like chart, and add pictures, art projects, and other items to the board as well.

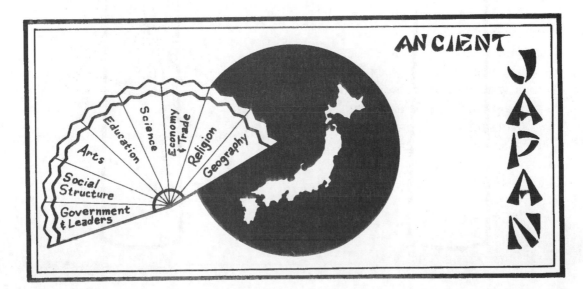

Torii Gates Outline

Cut large torii gates out of butcher paper to place around your classroom doors.

Bibliography

Fiction

Cassedy, Sylvia and Suetake Kunihiro, trans. *Red Dragonfly on My Shoulder.* HarperCollins, 1992.

Dalkey, Kara. *Little Sister.* Harcourt Brace, 1996.

Haugaard, Erik Christian. *The Boy and the Samurai.* Houghton Mifflin, 1991.

Haugaard, Erik Christian. *The Revenge of the Forty-Seven Samurai.* Houghton Mifflin, 1995.

Haugaard, Erik Christian. *The Samurai's Tale.* Houghton Mufflin, 1984.

Haviland, Virginia. *Favorite Fairy Tales Told in Japan.* Little Brown and Company, 1967.

Kawauchi, Sayumi. *Once Upon a Time in Japan.* Kodansha Publishers Ltd., 1987.

Martin, Rafe. *Mysterious Tales of Japan.* G. P. Putnam's Sons, 1996.

Paterson, Katherine. *The Master Puppeteer.* Thomas Y. Crowell Company, 1975.

Paterson, Katherine. *Of Nightingales That Weep.* Thomas Y. Crowell Company, 1974.

Paterson, Katherine. *The Sign of The Chrysanthemum.* Harper Trophy, 1973.

San Souci, Robert D. *The Samurai's Daughter.* Dial Books for Young Readers, 1992.

Uchida, Yoshiko. *The Magic Listening Cap: More Folk Tales from Japan.* Creative Arts Book Company, 1987.

Yagawa, Sumiko. *The Crane Wife.* William Morrow, 1981.

Nonfiction

Cobb, Vicki. *This Place Is Crowded.* Walker, 1992.

Galvin, Irene, Flum. *Japan, a Modern Land with Ancient Roots.* Benchmark Books, 1996.

Greene, Carol. *Japan, Enchantment of the World.* Children's Press, 1983.

Kidder, J. Edward. *Ancient Japan.* The John Day Company, 1997.

Morris, Ivan. *The World of the Shining Prince.* Alfred A. Knopf, 1964.

Neurath, Marie and Evelyn Worboys. *They Lived Like This in Ancient Japan.* Franklin Watts, Inc., 1966.

Odijk, Pamela. *The Japanese.* Silver Burdett, 1989.

Pilbeam, Mavis. *Japan.* Franklin Watts, 1988.

Pitts, Forrest Ralph. *Japan.* Gateway Press, 1988.

Shelley, Rex. *Japan, Cultures of the World.* Marshall Cavendish, 1994.

Zurlo, Tony. *Japan: Superpower of the Pacific.* Dillon Press, 1991.

Internet

The following Web sites contain information about Japanese history and culture:

http://www.jinjapan.org/kidsweb/
http://www.jinjapan.org/today/culture.html
http://www.fix.co.jp/kabuki/kabuki.html
http://sequoia.nttam.com/KIDS/
http://lcweb2.loc.gov/frd/cs/jptoc.html
http://www.theodora.com/wfb/japan_geography.html
http://www.us-japan.org/EdoMatsu/
http://www.wsu.edu:8080/~dee/ANCJAPAN/ANCJAPAN.HTM
http://www.culture-at-work.com/jpnlinks.html
http://www.japan-guide.com/e/e420.html
http://www.fcps.k12.va.us/DIT/eclass/japan1/japan1.htm

Answer Key

Page 9

1. J
2. Y
3. Y
4. Y, T
5. J
6. J
7. T
8. T
9. J
10. J
11. T
12. T
13. Y
14. Y
15. J

Page 10

1. Hokkaido
2. Honshu
3. Mount Fuji
4. Shikoku
5. Kyushu
6. Ryukyu
7. The Sea of Okhotsk
8. Pacific Ocean
9. East China Sea
10. Sea of Japan
11. Korea Strait

Page 14

Buddhism: D, F, H, L, M, N, Q
Shinto: B, C, E, G, I, J, K, O, P,
Both: A

Page 41

1. F
2. C
3. I
4. E
5. L
6. D
7. H
8. G
9. A
10. K
11. B
12. J

Page 47

1. Taika Reforms
2. Fujiwara
3. peasants
4. samurai
5. Bakufu
6. emperor
7. shogun
8. Kamakura
9. Daimyo
10. Ashikaga
11. Toyotomi Hideyoshi
12. Tokugawa Ieyasu
13. bushido
14. craftsmen
15. merchants